The most beautiful
Wine Villages of France

First published 2002
under the title: *Les Plus Beaux Villages du Vins de France*
by Flammarion 2002
Copyright © 2002 Archipel studio
10, rue Louis-Bertrand
94200 Ivry-sur-Seine

Copyright © Mitchell Beazley, 2005, for the English edition

ISBN: 1 84533 082 X

A CIP catalogue record for this book is available from the
British Library.

The author and publishers will be grateful for any information
which will assist them in keeping future editions up-to-date.
Although all reasonable care has been taken in the preparation
of this book, neither the publishers nor the author can accept
any liability for any consequences arising from the use thereof,
or the information contained therein.

Commissioning Editor Hilary Lumsden
Editors Sam Stokes, Jamie Ambrose
Translation Jennifer Patterson for Silva Editions Ltd

Typeset in New Baskerville and Formata
Printed in Italy

François Morel

The most beautiful
Wine Villages of France

MITCHELL BEAZLEY

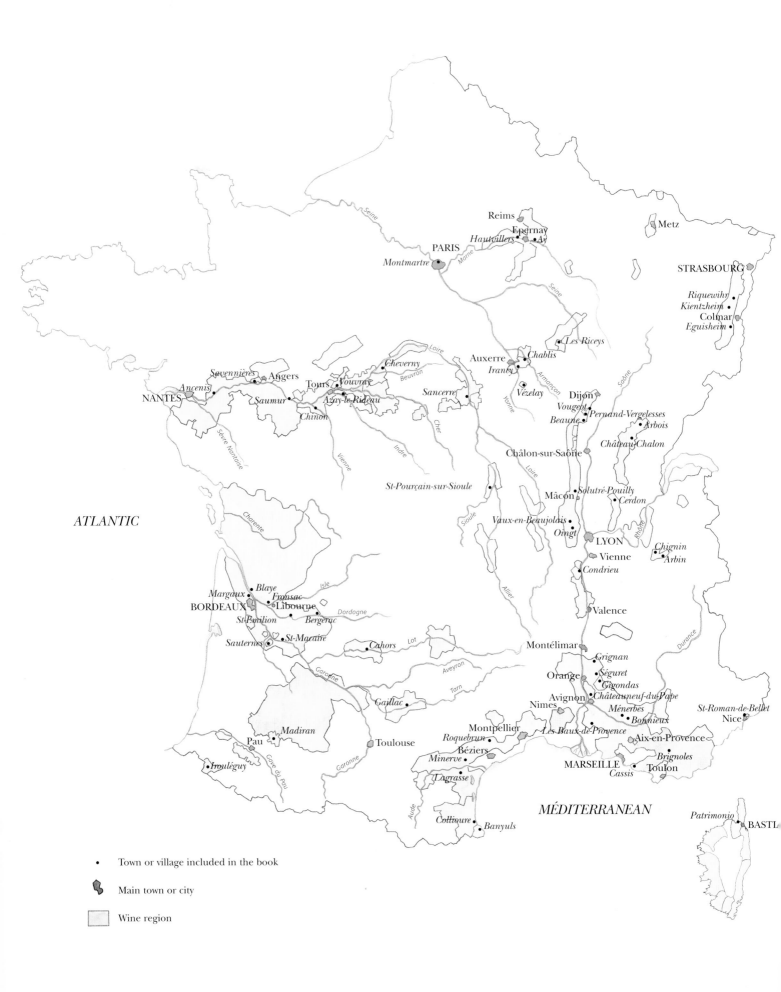

ATLANTIC

MÉDITERRANEAN

Reims
Metz
Épernay
Hautvillers   Aÿ
PARIS
Montmartre
STRASBOURG
Riquewihr
Kientzheim
Colmar
Eguisheim
Les Riceys
Auxerre   Chablis
Iranty
Savennières   Cheverny
Angers   Beuvron
Ancenis   Tours   Vouvray   Sancerre   Vézelay   Dijon
NANTES   Saumur   Azay-le-Rideau   Vougeot   Pernand-Vergelesses
Chinon   Beaune   Arbois
Château-Chalon
Châlon-sur-Saône
Sèvre Nantaise
St-Pourçain-sur-Sioule   Mâcon   Solutré-Pouilly
Cerdon
Charente   Vaux-en-Beaujolais
Oingt   LYON   Chignin
Vienne   Arbin
Condrieu
Blaye   Valence
Margaux   Fronsac
BORDEAUX   Libourne
St-Émilion   Bergerac   Montélimar   Grignan
Sauternes   St-Macaire   Orange   Séguret
Cahors   Gigondas
Châteauneuf-du-Pape
Nîmes   Ménerbes   St-Roman-de-Bellet
Madiran   Avignon   Bonnieux   Nice
Pau   Les Baux-de-Provence
Gaillac   Montpellier   Aix-en-Provence
Roquebrun
Irouléguy   Toulouse   Béziers   Brignoles
Minerve   MARSEILLE   Toulon
Lagrasse   Cassis
Gave du Pau   Patrimonio
Collioure   BASTI
Banyuls

•   Town or village included in the book

    Main town or city

    Wine region

Contents

Introduction

In essence, a wine is defined by the vineyard's terroir: the soil, the aspect, and the climate of the location. At least, that is the case for the genuine article. The very principle of French appellations (on wine labels or as regulatory guarantees) is rooted in the concept of origin, in the extraordinary diversity of climate, geology, and culture that forms part of each individual region. The many French ACs (*appellations contrôllées*), with their rich variety of names, incorporate everything from tiny hamlets to larger rural towns. Each boasts its own local architecture and proudly held traditions, making wine that is not just a product of the vine, but a history, a way of life, and an expression of the specific village where it was made.

You only have to walk through the streets of Kientzheim in Alsace, Turquant in the Loire Valley, Pernand-Vergelesses in Burgundy, Margaux in Bordeaux, Châteauneuf-du-Pape in the Rhône Valley, and Minerve in Languedoc-Roussillon to sense the deeply individual identity of these wines – even before discovering their flavour firsthand in the cellar of a local wine-grower.

The villages featured in the following pages have been chosen for their unique personalities and the way they typify the viticultural production of their region. Together, they outline the geography of the provinces and map the very soul of French wine. The specific vineyards will give a clear impression of the taste and flavour of individual wines and will make tangible the subtle and fleeting sensations of wine tasting, thereby enriching the wine-lover's enjoyment of all things fine and beautiful.

Through the vineyards of France

Our journey through French vineyards begins in Paris – a reminder that the Ile-de-France region was once one of the largest wine-producing areas in the country. The journey continues across provinces, along rows of vines on hillsides and valleys, beside major waterways and rivers, over plateaux and plains: places where, through the centuries, man has learned how to marry specific grape varieties to a particular soil.

Thus, Champagne's wide, open countryside is followed by the sloping plots of Alsatian hills. The mosaic of highly individual Burgundian microclimates precede the verdant villages of Beaujolais. The mountainous valleys and abrupt Jurassic foothills of Savoie are followed by the Rhône's fertile banks and the sunny Provençal countryside. The steep Languedoc and Roussillon escarpments lead onto the foothills of the Pyrénées, and those in turn onto the characteristic vineyards of the South West. The elegant hills of Bordeaux are followed by the luminous charm of the Loire and the rustic flavours of the centre of France, right up to St-Pourçain-sur-Sioule, the most astonishing among the first historic *crus* (named vineyards and their wine).

Along the way, the voyage will reveal many grape varieties which, through their wine, divulge the secrets of where they were grown, from prestigious places to little-known locations. As the novelist Colette said, "Vines and wine are both great mysteries. The vine is the only plant in the vegetable kingdom that allows us to taste the true flavour of the earth." And each village is a small and unique plot of that earth.

Château-Chalon embodies the riches of France's wine-growing lands, with an exceptional vineyard site alongside a modest village.

Montmartre

PARIS

Amid the vines of Montmartre and the hilltop houses, winemakers from an Anjou *confrérie* pay a fraternal visit during festivities in honour of the Greek wine god, Bacchus.

Today's Montmartre, bustling with shops and tourists along the steep, winding streets that lead up to the Sacré Coeur and Place du Tertre, bears little resemblance to days gone by. Before it was annexed to Paris in 1860 and integrated into the city's eighteenth *arrondissement* (civil district), this hilltop was home to a village called la Butte. A taste of the area's past is preserved by the Clos Montmartre, however, which was purchased and restored as a vineyard by the City of Paris in 1933.

Parisian wines

For a long time, Clos Montmartre was the only Parisian vineyard to enjoy a revival. Then, in 1983, it was joined by Clos des Morillons, a vineyard of Pinot Noir in the Parc de Georges-Brassens (fifteenth *arrondissement*) on the site of the Vaugirard abattoirs. Next came the vineyard of the Parc de Bercy (twelfth *arrondissement*), situated where the famous old wine warehouses used to stand, and finally, a vineyard was planted in the Parc de Belleville (twentieth district) overlooking the city of Paris. Not to be outdone, the Ile-de-France region can boast the Clos du Pas St-Maurice at Suresnes, the largest and most "serious" of the Ile-de-France wines, as well as the Argenteuil vineyard and many more. In fact, the vineyards are so numerous today that 30,000 bottles of "historic" wine are produced here annually, and the Association des Vignerons Franciliens Réunis (the association of reunited Île-de-France wine-growers) was founded in 2000 to act as a federation for these many vintners.

Parisian vineyards

Like many of the villages bordering Paris, Montmartre was once covered in vines. Indeed, its wine had enjoyed a good reputation ever since the beginning of the Middle Ages. The beverage was reputed to have unusual properties; as a seventeenth-century saying claimed, "This is Montmartre wine, whoever drinks a pint of it, pisses a quart!" (A pint was almost a litre and a quart was two pints.) In those days, the landscape featured vines, small houses, gardens, and windmills. In fact, all the mounds and hills of Paris and the surrounding Ile-de-France area were planted with vines, forming one of the largest French vineyards which stretched from the Montagne Ste-Geneviève to Vaugirard, and from Belleville and Charonne to Suresnes and Argenteuil. During the nineteenth century, however, vine disease, the growth of the railways and, most importantly, urban expansion ravaged these large vineyards. They only resurfaced during the twentieth century in the form of small, nostalgic plots.

The Clos Montmartre

The hilltop at Montmartre lost its rural appearance when it became the playground of bohemian artists and a paradise of cabarets and dancehalls, including the famous Lapin Agile. In 1933, however, a vineyard was replanted on the initiative of local painter Poulbot. The sloping plot is located at the corner of the Rue St-Vincent and the Rue des Saules, in the shadow of the huge Sacré Coeur basilica (built in 1875). Today, the vineyard is planted with 1,556 square metres (16,750 square feet) of Gamay, Pinot Noir, and other grape varieties, including hybrids. Sadly, the total of 1,762 individual vines don't make great wine, as the vineyard is north-facing. However, this was not the idea; the vines are there to uphold tradition and keep folklore alive. The harvest results in the sale of rare – and therefore costly – bottles of the vineyard's wine.

Ay

CHAMPAGNE

"Sparkling Ay glistens with the light of good fortune…" Alfred de Vigny, a nineteenth-century poet, refers to the sheer luck of this small but famous village for being fortuitously located in the very heart of the Champagne region. Nestled in between other terroirs of exceptional quality but different characteristics, Ay is in a remarkably privileged spot on the right bank of the Marne, in the middle of the vineyards bordering the valley at the southern end of the Montagne de Reims vineyard, and just opposite the start of the Côte des Blancs on the left bank.

Winemaking became the predominant activity in this village early on, and wines "from the river" referred precisely to the wines of Ay. These wines were originally a pale red in colour, and were highly esteemed in Paris and the north long before their colour became standardized as white – and before its effervescent style had been mastered: the style that would become known as Champagne.

The spire of Ay's bell tower reaches high into the Champagne sky (*right*) at the foot of vineyards that scale the surrounding hillsides (*far right*).

A prestigious centre

According to Henri IV's doctor, the amiable Framboisière, the wines of Ay "rank right at the top on account of their goodness and perfection". They assured Ay's great reputation, which is evident today throughout the village. The ramparts themselves can now only be seen from the layout of the boulevards and a few other remains around the famous Clos Chaudes Terres of Bollinger – planted with rare "old French vines" of ungrafted Pinot Noir – but the history of the village can be read from the ancient houses that line the streets. Enclosed inner courtyards speak of a time when attack was likely, their narrow passages rendering them almost impenetrable. Henri IV's press-house lurks in the shadow of a beautiful Gothic church – a prime example of that flamboyant style – and François I's press-house and chamberlain's house are still standing. Gosset is by far the oldest Champagne house in the village, dating from 1584.

The marvellous nineteenth-century town houses bordering the rue Jeanson bear witness to the more recent prosperity of the Champagne companies and traders who have set up in Ay throughout the years. One of these buildings, known as the Villa Bissinger, is today the headquarters of the Institut International des Vins de Champagne (International Institute of Champagne Wines).

Top terroir

The Champagne index rates the vineyards of Ay at no less than 100 per cent. This score relates the value of the harvest to the maximum price fixed by the trade. The village comprises one of seventeen *grands crus* which, together with forty-one *premiers crus*, are scattered exclusively between the Marne Valley, the Montagne de Reims, and the Côte des Blancs of Champagne. The black grape varieties, Pinot Noir and Pinot Meunier, largely dominate the planting at Ay, leaving only a little room for Chardonnay and several "forgotten" but nonetheless interesting grapes such as Petit Meslier. As with all good terroirs of the Champagne region, the soil of Ay is characterized by a deep layer of porous, chalky limestone, which acts as an excellent heat and moisture regulator. It also, of course, makes an ideal building material for the Champagne cellars!

Hautvillers

CHAMPAGNE

Hautvillers is famed for the magnificient signs of its wine-growers, especially those made by the Babé ironworks at Cramant.

Hautvillers is the historic and the symbolic heart of Champagne. The village boasts a dominant position on the hillside of the river Marne's right bank, opposite the town of Epernay and on the southern limits of the Montagne de Reims. Founded in the seventh century, its Benedictine abbey was destined to play an important role from the start, as its workshop of scribes and illuminators was a magnet for artists in the Carolingian era. From early on, wines "from the river" were distinguished from those "of the mountain", which came from the northern slopes

Dom Pérignon

Dom Pérignon, the procurator and cellarer of the Hautvillers abbey during the middle of Louis XIV's reign, played a key role in the perfection of Champagne. Although he is not actually its inventor (as a popular legend claimed after his death), he nonetheless succeeded in controlling both its colour and effervescence and in improving the quality of the *vin de base*: the base wine. After forty-seven years of hard work in Champagne, we can thank Dom Pérignon for the choice of grape varieties, with a preference for Pinot Noir; grape selection during harvest; subtle gathering and blending of grapes from various different terroirs; rapid pressing to leave the juice white; fermentation in a cool cellar, such as the one he had dug out of the rock on the track to Cumières; and decanting and fining and bottling in thick, English-style glass.

of the Montagne de Reims. The river wines were considered to be among the best in "France" – that is to say in the Ile-de-France region – long before the idea of a Champagne appellation came into being.

Dom Pérignon country

It took centuries for the pale-grey or light-red wines to develop into what we call Champagne. It was not until the end of the seventeenth century that Dom Pérignon and the monks of the Abbey of St-Pierre at Hautvillers mastered their theories on winemaking and accepted the vital fizzy

characteristic that would rapidly see it recognized and appreciated throughout the world. Most of the history and legend surrounding this festive wine hail from Hautvillers and its austere abbey.

Today, after various reconstructions, only an abbey church remains, a simple parish church built in the sixteenth and seventeenth centuries. Inside, two tombstones tell the tale of Champagne's viticultural history: that of Dom Pérignon and his friend Dom Ruinart, who rediscovered the underground Gallo-Roman *crayères* of Reims and developed them as cellars for the effervescent wine. The monastic buildings became the property of Moët et Chandon. The atmosphere in the village of Hautvillers is the epitome of the Champagne region. Historic buildings are of a plain yet grand style combining local chalk with brick, and basket-arch gateways are decorated with wrought-iron signs. The sloping streets offer beautiful views over the river Marne as well as of the surrounding vineyards as far as Cumières and Dizy. Here, as with all the wine-growing villages of Champagne, the surroundings speak of the hard work that goes into the production of this wine. Only after skilled hard work and a long wait can the party begin…

The Benedictine Abbey of Hautvillers, made famous by Dom Pérignon, is one of the highlights of the Champagne vineyard.

Les Riceys

In Les Riceys, everything comes in threes. The village itself is in fact made up of three parts: Ricey-Bas (Lower Ricey), Ricey-Haut-Rive (Ricey Upper Bank), and Ricey-Haut (Upper Ricey). Each area is defined by its relationship with the Laignes, the small tributary of the Seine that waters the lush valley. This commune (France's smallest administrative unit) is the most important of Champagne's wine-growing areas and is the only one to contain three separate appellations: Champagne, for its sparkling wine; Coteaux Champenois, for its still wine; and Rosé des Riceys for the exclusive local specialty, which is also still.

This rosé is a traditional wine that has been carefully preserved so that it is probably close to the original style of wine from Champagne, *i.e.* still rosé. Production requires a high degree of skill, especially in an area almost exclusively preoccupied with making sparkling wine. Its existence, therefore, remains relatively rare and

secret, but it is famous among those in the know as one of the best and certainly most original French rosés.

Historical Riceys

Les Riceys is located in the south of the Aube, where the provinces of Champagne and Burgundy meet; both Tonnerre and Chablis are nearby. The undulating countryside here was incorporated

Riceys rosé

Production of Riceys rosé is a risky business. Of the 886 wine-producing hectares of the commune, only the 350 best south-facing slopes are suitable. In reality, however, just thirty-five or forty hectares of Pinot Noir – the only permitted variety – are reserved for this local specialty, and even then, only in the good years. The grower has to declare to the National Institute for the Designation of Origin (INAO) which plots will be used so that these may be inspected and approved. Healthy grapes and a potential alcohol level of at least ten degrees are mandatory. Once the wine has been made, it has to undergo official tasting that will grant – or refuse – the Rosé des Riceys appellation. The wine is made by a brief maceration of the grapes and a rapid and carefully supervised fermentation that lasts just a few days. It has to be removed from the vats as soon as as it attains a cherry-pink colour and at precisely the moment when the "Riceys flavour" is judged to be perfect. The flavour contains hints of cherry, strawberry, raspberry, redcurrant, and violet, with a touch of almond and hazelnut.

into the Champagne wine-growing area at the start of the twentieth century and is a mixture of vineyards, grassland, and woodland that create unique, natural characteristics for wine-growing.

The small town boasts an abundance of historic churches, such as the imposing church of Ricey-Bas, dating back to the thirteenth century, the elegant sixteenth-century church of Ricey-Haute-Rive, and the unusual church of Ricey-Haut, dating from the fifteenth and sixteenth centuries. The Ricey-Bas château combines both classical and medieval architecture, and there are numerous tiny chapels scattered over the commune. There are also more modest buildings called the *cadoles*. These are old, dry-stone shelters whose primitive silhouettes are dotted around the vineyards, adding charm to the small valleys and byways.

The background of vine-filled hillsides and wooded crests makes the perfect backdrop for Les Riceys' stone architecture.

Eguisheim

ALSACE

Surrounded by vines, its streets bordered by half-timbered buildings (*right*), Eguisheim is one of the most picturesque villages in Alsace.

Eguisheim holds a special place in the metaphorical garland of flower-filled villages that line the foothills of the Vosges, each more colourful than the last. The historical village and its vineyards look out across the Alsace plain towards Colmar and form such a picture-perfect image of Alsace that the scene could have been torn out of a sketchbook by the late-nineteenth/early twentieth-century designer and illustrator Hansi (Jean Jacques Waltz). But it is far more than merely picturesque. Around the turn of the first millennium, the name "Eguisheim" was already at the head of a list of 160 villages in Alsace that are now famous for producing wine.

Stronghold of the Alsatian vineyards

Eguisheim was once the seat of a powerful count who made sure his walled city was secure within its ramparts. An octagonal, medieval castle, which holds an important place in Alsatian history, and a church with a Romanesque bell tower form the heart of the village. The streets wind away from this tightly packed enclosure in a series of concentric circles, passing concealed courtyards and small squares, half in the sunshine and half in the shade. The narrow, half-timbered houses were built in a dense network with high, painted cob walls.

Outside Eguisheim's entrance gates, the vineyards themselves conquer the hillside that climbs up behind the houses and the huge plots that run down to the plain. Naturally, the slopes provide the best terroirs, notably those of the reputable *grands crus* Eichberg and Pfersigberg, under the protection of the Trois Châteaux d'Eguisheim that crown the wooded summit of the Schlossberg hill. The châteaux were originally three donjons, the massive remains of the towers of three medieval castles (Weckmund, Wahlenbourg, and Dagsbourg) that once watched over the valley from this elevated position. They still dominate today's skyline, imposing their symbolic silhouettes on the surrounding vineyards and villages.

Aside from the medieval remains, another feature of this Alsatian countryside is its much-visited cooperative cellars. In a region where collectivity has played a determining role, Eguisheim's wine cellar, built in 1902, used to be one of the best in Alsace, and today remains the largest. Various tasting cellars in Eguisheim also offer merry Alsatian hospitality to wine-lovers.

Which grape where?

The diverse terroirs of the Alsatian vineyards allow various grape varieties to be grown successfully side by side. Eguisheim's *grands crus* offer a good example. Leichberg, a terroir with a calcareous clay marl facing southeast in a relatively sheltered site, has a particularly warm and dry microclimate well-suited to Gewurztraminer, but also to Riesling and Tokay-Pinot Gris. Its wines are both refined and full-bodied. Pfersigberg, which is more calcareous, faces east-southeast and favours an early-ripening grape. Its terroir is therefore best for Gewurztraminer but it also suits Riesling, producing rich and elegant wines.

Kientzheim

ALSACE

Squares, wells, and ancient dwellings make Kientzheim's charm unique among the many winemaking villages at the foot of the vine-clad hills (*right*).

For over four centuries, both visitors and invaders have been greeted by the outstretched tongue of Kientzheim's "Lallakenig" or "Lalli", a sculpture on the east gate of the village. The humour of this gesture is soon balanced, however, by the towering majesty of Kientzheim's château, filled with memories of the Counts of Lupfen, and the famous local hero, Lazare de Schwendi. The château is now the headquarters of the all-powerful St-Etienne Corporation, and houses the informative Musée du Vignoble et des Vins d'Alsace (Alsace Vineyards and Wine Museum). The town is

Tokay or Pinot Gris?

A persistent legend claims that, in the sixteenth century, after a campaign against the Turks, Lazare de Schwendi brought Tokay vines from Hungarian vineyards to Kientzheim. However, this is simply not the case. The Alsatian grapes bear no relation to any of the varieties that make the outstanding wine on the hills of Tokaji. Rather, they come from Pinot Gris, planted in old French vineyards, and formerly called "Fromenteau" in Champagne and the

"Ile-de-France" or "Pinot Beurot" in Burgundy. Nonetheless, the first mention of this variety in Alsace appears in documents related to fining at Kientzheim. Today, it is one of the four "nobles" of the Alsatian vineyards. Ripening early, it gives rich, spicy wines that are well-rounded and oily, yet it is also particularly well-suited to Vendange Tardive (late-harvested wines) and to the Sélection des Grains Nobles (luxury nobly rotten wines).

encircled by a fourteenth-century wall and is located on the Weiss Valley road, between the villages of Kaysersberg and Sigolsheim.

Surrounded by grapes

In the middle of Kientzheim stands a partly Gothic church that shelters the tomb of Lazare de Schwendi, whom legend credits with the introduction of the Tokay grape variety. The Tour des Bourgeois ("Townspeople's Tower") lies to the west of town and the Tour des Voleurs ("Thieves' Tower") to the east. The towers, along with the

wealthy houses, small squares, and wells, all contribute to the timeless charm of the place. The hills surrounding Kientzheim are covered with vines and crowned with woodland.

In 1975, the Riesling terraces of Schlossberg became the first recognized *grand cru* of Alsace. The vineyards reach right up to the imposing tower of Kaysersberg's medieval castle, which, along with a fortified bridge over the Weiss, make Kaysersberg one of the most characteristically Alsatian places of the region. Gewurztraminer and Tokay-Pinot Gris thrive in the Furstentum

Grand Cru; warm and well-sheltered, it is also a surprisingly suitable climate for Mediterranean plants. Above Sigolsheim, Mambourg is almost entirely given over to lush, abundant Gewurztraminer grapes. Grafreben and Altenbourg share the same slopes and embrace the banks of the Weiss, as at Patergarten between Kientzheim and Kaysersberg. The many different terroirs and various grape varieties around Kientzheim are so diverse that, if a symphony were written in celebration of Alsatian wine, they would comprise the best movement of the score.

Riquewihr

ALSACE

Surrounded by a sea of vines, Riquewihr is the true heart of the Alsatian wine region. Firstly, it lies right in the middle of the wine route that wends its way from Thann in the south up to Marlenheim in the north, through the many hillside villages beneath the Vosges Mountains. Secondly, it plays an important role in Alsace's viticultural history.

Museum village

The whole town of Riquewihr has been awarded Monument Historique (national heritage site) status and is recognized as a living museum. The historical architecture includes quadrangular late thirteenth-century fortifications such as the Tour du Dolder and the Tour des Voleurs, the old prison. Also of interest are its half-timbered façades, curving tiled roofs, galleried courtyards, oriels (an upper-storey bay with a window), fountains, and wells.

The entire town of Riquewihr – streets, byways, squares, and statues – is a designated national heritage site.

During its wealthiest period – the sixteenth and seventeenth centuries – Riquewihr acquired treasures such as the Wertemberg ducal château,

Terroirs and varieties

Unlike most French regions, Alsatian wines are defined by their grape varieties. Since 1975, in order to protect the age-old reputation of its better terroirs, Alsace has also defined around fifty-one *grands crus* where the quality of the soil and exposure is ideally suited to one – or several – of the four "noble" Alsatian grape varieties: Riesling, Gewurztraminer, Tokay-Pinot Gris, and Muscat. When conditions are favourable, these *grands crus* can excel themselves, but Riquewihr's Schoenenbourg has the highest potential for excellence, both with its Vendange Tardive and its Sélection des Grains Nobles, referring to the successive picking of grapes affected by noble rot.

Riquewihr's brilliantly
coloured half-timbered
buildings and metal signs
contribute towards making
it a veritable living museum.

and most importantly, a group of houses
that form a wonderful ensemble of traditional
Alsatian domestic architecture.

Riquewihr's pedigree

From early times, Riquewihr has been known
for the quality of its terroirs and for its
uncompromising *vignerons*. North of the village,
Riesling, the great Rhine grape, has superb
results on the south-facing slopes of the famous
Grand Cru Schoenenbourg. To the southeast,
Grand Cru Sporen's gentler inclines are
particularly favourable for Gewurztraminer
and Tokay-Pinot Gris. For centuries, these
two prestigious *crus* have been the jewels
in the Alsatian vineyards' crown.

With top-quality terroirs such
as Schoenenbourg – which
reaches the foot of the town's
fortifications – Riquewihr is justly
called "the pearl of the vineyard".

Beaune

BURGUNDY

Beaune is the prestigious wine capital of Burgundy, and wine has been made and sold here since very early days. The name "Beaune" evokes the ancient patronage of Belenos, the Celtic god of the sun. For many years, the hillside wines of the Côte d'Or area were named after the city, until they acquired a Burgundian identity at the beginning of the fifteenth century.

Today, Beaune is still identified with the southern part of this wine-growing area and with the vineyards that lie to the west of the town. As the ducal capital, it played an important role in the expansion of Burgundy before being replaced by Dijon. But most importantly, its greatest claim to fame is that it has remained the true capital of wine; since the eighteenth century, important négociants have established and developed their trade here at Beaune. Today, the négociants are more prosperous than ever and many have become vineyards owners themselves.

Baskets overflowing with bunches of Pinot Noir grapes at harvest time is a timeless spectacle in Beaune.

The "capital"

Beaune is rich in period architecture that speaks of its importance through history. Visitors can still see the twelfth-century ramparts around the town with their fifteenth- and sixteenth-century additions. Strong walls, towers, and bastions also remain – most of them owned by the larger Beaune wine-trading companies. The old moat has been transformed into gardens, and a fifteenth-century castle with two towers still intact on the east wall. At the heart of the tightly packed, concentric network of streets, the collegiate church of Notre-Dame watches over the town. This building is a fine example of Burgundy's Romanesque architecture and has some Gothic additions to boot.

Around almost every corner of every street in the citadel there is evidence of Beaune's prosperity through the centuries: Renaissance town houses, most notably that of the Dukes of Burgundy with its Gothic cellar, now the Musée du Vin de Bourgogne (the wine museum); monasteries and convents, such as that of the Ursulines, dating from the seventeenth century, now home to the town hall; the Musée des Beaux-Arts (the art museum), and the Musée Etienne-Jules-Marey (a museum of early photography); antique dwellings; and a thousand secret courtyards, gardens, cellars, stairways, passages…

There are also treasures to be found outside the walls. In the *vignerons* district, to the north of the town, historical houses are grouped around the thirteenth-century church of St-Nicolas. From the bell tower, with its typical slender spire, the tolling would have rung out across the lower slopes of Beaune's mountain in this area known locally as "the kidney of the *côte*", where a string of special *crus*, such as Grèves and Cent Vignes, are located.

The Hospices

Beaune is famous throughout the world for the annual charity event that takes place in the city's architectural masterpiece, the Hôtel Dieu. The exquisite building was formerly a general hospital,

With its roofs richly decorated in glazed tiles, the Hospices de Beaune symbolizes the old towns of Burgundy.

The Côte de Beaune is totally covered in vines, a dense network of plots arranged according to the slopes.

forming the main part of a religious hospice. Founded in the middle of the fifteenth century by Nicolas Rolin (chancellor to the Duke of Burgundy) and his wife, Guigone de Salins, to take care of the sick and impoverished, it is now a much-visited museum. The appeal of the grand building lies in its inspirational Flemish style and the extraordinarily colourful tapestry of glazed ceramic tiles that line the roof of the inner courtyard. The entrance, endowed with a plain façade and surmounted by a tall steeple, is the

Beaune and its appellation

The AC of Beaune has many different microclimates. The Côte de Beaune extends beyond the western horizon, ending at Mont Battois, otherwise known as Beaune's "mountain". Between Savigny-lès-Beaune in the north and Pommard in the south, forty-one *premiers crus* occupy the middle of the hill slopes. These are planted mostly with Pinot Noir grapes but leave a little room for Chardonnay grapes to make white wine. The individual terroirs facing the town form a string of evocative names: Clos du Roi, Marconnets, Cent Vignes, Fèves, Bressandes, Grèves – and in the middle, the famous Vigne de l'Enfant Jésus – Teurons, Champs Pimont, Avaux; Boucherottes, and the Clos des Mouches, famous for its white wine.

only part that is tiled in plain slate. The impressive Grande Salle, or "invalids' room", within has twenty-eight columned beds and an oratory where Roger van der Weyden's famous triptych, the *Last Judgement*, used to hang. (It is now in a nearby room.) Since the charitable institution was built, it

has been financed solely by donations of vines that now make up a vineyard of sixty-one hectares, mostly originating in the Côte de Beaune. The annual sale of these wines, famous for their prestigious origins and donors, such as Beaune Premier Cru les Cent Vignes "Nicolas Rolin", is a unique event that draws professional négociants and amateur wine enthusiasts alike from all over the world and sets the prices for the season. This public auction takes place by candlelight on the third Sunday in November, and is the highlight of a three-day wine festival known as Beaune's *Trois Glorieuses*.

The medieval appearance is well-preserved, from the city's layout and collegiate church to the Hospices.

Chablis

BURGUNDY

The famous vineyards of Chablis lie in a pastoral setting on the banks of the river Serein.

Following the waters that flow through the valleys between the Côte d'Or and Champagne to meet at the Yonne before it flows into the Seine, the vineyards of lower Burgundy enjoy a particularly special terroir. Undeniably, the most perfect expression of this is found in the pale golden hue and green glints of Chablis.

The work of monks

For centuries, local monks have known how to get the best out of the gently sloping banks of the river Serein that are so well-suited to the cultivation of vines. The first to develop them were Benedictines in the ninth century, who, fleeing the invading Normans, came here from St Martin's Abbey in Tours.

Their founding role was recalled in the twelfth- and thirteenth-century with the construction of a collegial church dedicated to St Martin and

The great white grape of Burgundy

The vineyards and nineteen villages of the Chablis AC are situated in a relatively northerly situation, where severe spring frosts sometimes necessitate the placing of heaters or sprinkling systems between the rows to protect the vines. The terroirs cover some 4,000 hectares, composed of essentially chalky-clay Kimmeridge marl, which are planted with the great white Burgundy grape, Chardonnay. From the simplest to the most complex, the wines are divided into four appellations: Petit Chablis (505 hectares), Chablis (2,715 hectares), Chablis Premier Cru (740 hectares), and Chablis Grand Cru (103 hectares). The seven *grands crus* occupy one slope on the right bank of the Serein: Bougros, Preuses, Vaudésir, Grenouilles, Valmur, Les Clos, and Blanchots. The forty or so *premiers crus*, usually reorganized into seventeen, are divided between the right bank (Mont de Milieu, Montée

de Tonnerre, Fourchaume, etc.) and the left (Montmains, Vaillons, etc.) Fresh, lively wines, with citrus, herbal, and mineral notes, the better Chablis appellations evolve slowly, gaining honey and waxy nuances with field mushroom and woody undertones.

built in the same Gothic style as Sens Cathedral. The Cistercians were the next monks to make their mark upon Chablis' wine development by introducing Chardonnay grapes, the variety that without doubt flourishes best in this terrain.

The monks also selected prime designated sites that still comprise today's *grands crus* and *premiers crus.* They founded Pontigny Abbey in 1114, and it became famed far and wide as a shining centre of Cistercian wine production in Burgundy. Built a few kilometres north of the town, the abbey is a marvellously simple, powerful building.

In Chablis itself, Petit-Pontigny was a dependency of the abbey that managed a huge estate until the French Revolution, as is evident from the large press used for bulk processing.

Today, the cellar is the only remaining part of the original twelfth-century outbuildings. The Cistercians "invented" Chablis as it is known, securing the prosperity of the small town that has given its name to the most famous dry white wine in the world.

Small wine-producing villages are dotted among the vineyards throughout the valleys of Chablis.

Irancy

BURGUNDY

The seemingly calm, sinuous river Yonne has shaped the countryside of the *département* that bears its name. Its waters have carved out a channel among limestone rocks, at times impressive for their towering heights and deep caves. The river weaves among comfortably rounded hills and villages peaceably huddled around churches.

At Cravant, where the Cure swells the banks of the Yonne, the Auxerre vineyard begins. Due to the quality of the terroir, this vineyard – like all those of lower Burgundy – was for a long time reputedly equal to that of Beaune.

Vale of vines

On the right bank of the Yonne, near Vincelottes – a small port that was once devoted to transporting barrels of wine – lies Irancy. The village nestles in the centre of a natural amphitheatre formed by a large valley covered in vines. Some traces of the sixteenth-century inhabitants remain, such as a ring of promenades built on former defensive ditches at the foot of the slopes, which are now lined with lime trees. In this limestone country, the older houses all have cool, humid cellars dug out of the rock – perfectly adapted for winemaking.

The local eighteenth-century architect Soufflot used stone from the nearby quarry at Bailly when he built the Panthéon in Paris. (The quarry has now become an underground

Typical of the wine-growing villages of the Yonne, Irancy lies at the heart of a natural amphitheatre of planted vines.

A young AC and an ancient grape

In 1998, the Bourgogne Irancy appellation became Irancy AC. The 150 hectares of Pinot Noir, which produce rounded, elegant, and fruity wines, joined the ranks of the "great and famous": the appellations of the communes of the Côte d'Or that already included Chablis. What makes Irancy unique from these, however, is that it contains a small percentage of César – also called Romain – an old grape variety that dates from the time of Roman colonization.In fact, its characteristic leaves are sculpted on a second-century Gallo-Roman frieze that was found during archaeological excavations at Escolives-Ste-Camille on the other bank of the Yonne, just opposite Irancy.

cathedral-sized storage facility for Crémant de Bourgogne.)

The geometrical plots of vines that square off the surrounding slopes mirror the chequered tiled roofs of the village, whose uniformity is disturbed only by the square bell tower of the church. The vineyards are punctuated by cherry trees, which were another local specialty for a period of time. The best-placed slopes, which suit the Pinot Noir variety traditional to Burgundy, face south and west. These are the most sought-after microclimates, whose names include: Boudardes, Paradis, Mazelots, Côte du Moutie, and on the edge of the *côte* heading towards Cravant, the famous Palotte.

Houses built of local stone with tiled roofs cluster around the village centre at the foot of a vineyard studded with cherry trees.

Pernand-Vergelesses

BURGUNDY

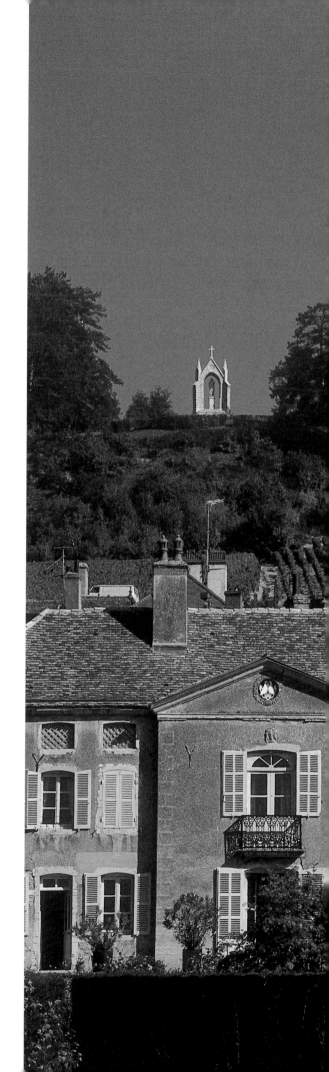

One of the magical wine-producing places of Burgundy, Pernand-Vergelesses sits in a narrow valley between the Corton mountain and the two round, forested summits called Bois Noël. Many a prestigious vineyard can be found across this landscape, where a combination of red and white wines are produced, including *grands crus*, *premiers crus*, and named *village* appellations.

Corton rises just beyond the Côte des Pierres, which separates the Côte de Nuits and the Côte de Beaune. The magical mixture of rural simplicity, *crus* and villages, and the infinite subtlety of the vineyards' terroirs is what that makes this region a beautiful place.

Below the mountain

Pernand-Vergelesses is almost hidden behind the famous Corton mountain. It is situated a little further back in the *côte* than both Ladoix-Serrigny, which reaches onto the plain on the road to Beaune at the eastern foot of Corton, and Aloxe-Corton, which is halfway up the slope to the south.

Built on the top of the Frétille hillside, Pernand-Vergelesses looks down over Corton's western flank towards the intermingled vineyards of Corton and Corton-Charlemagne. It typifies the wine-growing villages of Beaune, protected beneath the nineteenth-century Notre-Dame-de-Bonne-Espérance Oratory, and set close to the spring of Mère Fontaine,

The former house of Jacques Copeau's theatre company, the village church and, on top of the hill, the Notre-Dame-de-Bonne-Espérance Oratory.

Lords of red and white wine

In this northern part of the Côte de Beaune, the colour of the *cru*, whether red or white, depends on the variable proportions of chalk and clay in the soil and on which direction a plot faces. Uniquely, Grand Cru Corton is the only red to rival the Côte de Nuits, while Grand Cru Corton-Charlemagne, with its well-rounded personality, is the first of a long line of famous Beaune white wines that continue further south. The *premiers crus* of AC Pernand-Vergelesses – the Vergelesses, Ile des Vergelesses, and Fichots, etc. – make use of Chardonnay and of Pinot Noir, which are full-bodied and elegant at the same time.

which, along with its vantage point on the
hilltop, made it an ideal place to settle.

The picturesque Burgundian houses have
deep cellars that offer the perfect condition
for storing wine. Its sloping streets form a tightly
woven network around a Romanesque church
complete with a chevron-patterned spire. When
the sun reflects off the varnished roof tiles, the
spire looks as if it has been set alight. The place
was certainly inspirational for the theatre
producer Jacques Copeau, who rehearsed
here in the 1920s.

Shared crus

Facing south, the village has uninterrupted views
over the vines that parade up and down both
sides of the valley. Mostly belonging to Aloxe
before flowing over into Ladoix-Serrigny, the
plots facing west-southwest on the mountainside
produce the prestigious Corton-Charlemagne
and Corton wines. Those that face east-southeast
and run up to Savigny-lès-Beaune belong to
Bois Noël and produce the best Pernand *crus*.

Sheltered in a deep valley
in the *côte*, the village of
Pernand-Vergelesses is
surrounded by woodland
and vineyards.

Vézelay

BURGUNDY

The picturesque streets of Vézelay climb the slopes of the village's "eternal hill", drawing all manner of curious visitors.

The streets of Vézelay still resonate with the sound of footsteps from the past and the whole village is a UNESCO World Heritage Site. Through the years, pilgrims have passed by on their journey to Santiago de Compostella; crusaders have marched through, bound for the Second and Third Crusades; and Christians have gathered here since the Middle Ages.

Today, the streets throng with crowds of tourists, and their interest in the place has encouraged the replanting of the vines that once covered the lands, but which had almost completely disappeared by the end of the nineteenth century.

Rebirth of a vineyard

At just 100 hectares, the vineyard at Vézelay is modest in size. It is also young and was only replanted in the 1970s after phylloxera destroyed the vines many years before. It has a wine history, however, as the "Clos Dû" at Nanchèvres, a hamlet of St-Père, was previously the "Clos du Duc": a walled vineyard belonging to the Dukes of Burgundy. It also has links to ancient Roman times, as the remains of a temple to the wine god Bacchus were discovered under the old church of St-Etienne. Most of the wines produced at Vézelay are white, using the great Burgundy grape, Chardonnay, and bearing the Bourgogne Vézelay AC on their labels. The small amount of red produced from Pinot Noir comes under the simple Bourgogne AC. There is also a rare and more unusual wine, Bourgogne Blanc Grand Ordinaire, produced from the Melon de Bourgogne grape. This traditional old variety, often forgotten in its native land, reigns triumphant around Nantes under the name of Muscadet.

The eternal hillside

For eleven centuries, a monastery has reigned over the lush hills that border the river Cure. The large abbey church was built between the eleventh and thirteenth centuries to crown the so-called "eternal hill" in response to the growing power of this Christian meeting ground. After the French Revolution, the Church of the Madeleine almost fell into

ruin, but architect Eugène Emmanuel Viollet-le-Duc decided to restore it during the nineteenth century.

The vast building is a great attraction for visitors, admired for its Romanesque and Gothic architecture and above all, for its rich sculptural detail. With stylized, elongated figures clad in finely chiselled, almost lightweight draperies, the stone carvings on the capitals and the three doorways that lead into the nave pay homage to the elegance of Burgundian art.

The terrace of the former château behind the church offers splendid views over the Cure Valley. The streets and houses of the old town run in the opposite direction, towards the west, and are surrounded by ramparts dotted with towers and gates. At the foot of the ramparts below the abbey church, the vineyards stretch out across the hillside towards the neighbouring villages, St-Père-sous-Vézelay and Asquins, and towards Tharoiseau on the right bank of the river Cure.

Like the Auxerre, Joigny, and Tonnerre regions, this area is gradually rediscovering the vigour that it enjoyed in the golden heyday of wines from lower Burgundy.

From the top of its famous abbey church, Vézelay overlooks the surrounding countryside of vineyards, fields, and wooded hills.

Vougeot

BURGUNDY

The prestigious Chevaliers du Tastevin have their headquarters at the Château du Clos Vougeot (*right*).

The Vouge River rises in the middle of the Côte de Nuits and winds its way through the forest of Cîteaux on its way down to the river Saône, where it skirts the abbey founded in the early twelfth century. Here, in the dawn of the great Cistercian enterprise, the history of Burgundy's vineyards began when the monks of Cîteaux started to cultivate grapes on the banks of the river. Leaving the summit of the hill to the trees that crowned it, they chose the best sections of the mid-slopes – those that were sheltered from cold winds and enjoy the morning sun. At the foot of the vineyards, the small village of Vougeot sits on the edge of the river after which it was named.

In the sixteenth century, a bridge was built to attract trade from the other side of the river to the village's hostelries and inns. Despite its small size, Vougeot became the most famous name of the Côte de Nuits.

The clos and its château

The large, famous *clos* (walled vineyard) is at the very top of the wine hierarchy. For nine centuries the Clos Vougeot (or Clos de Vougeot) has been a shining example of the potential genius of Burgundy's *vignerons*. It is the smallest commune of the *côte*, with several houses in typical regional style gathered around a nineteenth-century church. The vineyard comprises fifty hectares that were painstakingly assembled, plot by plot, by monks in the Middle Ages, and enclosed by walls in the fourteenth century. Marvellous Romanesque buildings with large roofs stand in the middle of the vines. The half-buried cellar and the fermentation building, a real wine "cloister" endowed with four massive lever presses, are in the upper part of the *clos*.

It is unusual to find a château among the vines in the Burgundy countryside. The one that stands beside these buildings was built in the sixteenth century. Vast and austere, with two short, square towers, it blends very happily with this prestigious southern terroir. From well before the French Revolution until the end of the nineteenth century, the sixty plots of Clos de Vougeot were undivided.

Today, however, they belong to some seventy or eighty proprietors and vary enormously in both size and quality. The proportion of clay or chalk in the soil varies, with those in the upper and middle areas reputed to be superior to those in the lower parts. In the shadow of the Grand Cru Clos de Vougeot several *premiers crus* complete the status of this village, which is almost entirely devoted to Pinot Noir: Clos de la Perrière, Cras, Petits Vougeots, and the unique Clos Blanc, totally given over to Chardonnay grapes.

The Chevaliers du Tastevin

Created in Nuits-St-Georges in 1934, the Chevaliers du Tastevin is the most famous of all wine-growers' associations and has owned the Château du Clos Vougeot since 1944. This is where the authoritative chapter meetings are held, as well as the *tastevinage*: tastings that select the best Côte d'Or wines. Each year on the third Saturday in November, the association holds the historic reunion of its members, after tasting the burgundies due to be auctioned the next day at the Hospices de Beaune.

Solutré-Pouilly

MÂCON

At the foot of the massive Roche de Solutré (*right*), vines and villages occupy the large slopes characteristic of the Mâcon landscape.

Crowned by sheer cliffs about 100 metres (328 feet) tall, the Roche de Solutré, a limestone outcrop 493 metres (1,617 feet) high, towers in the midst of the hill slopes and valleys that mould the south Mâcon countryside. From the top it is possible to see over the entire Saône Valley to the Juras Mountains and the Alps beyond.

The Roche de Vergisson, a twin outcrop to the north, and the Mont de Pouilly hill emphasize the powerful undulations of the terrain. The soil is pale golden or reddish and contrasts with the grey rocks and green vegetation. The villages set in the middle of their vineyards are dwarfed by this vast "decor".

Solutré: a long history

The history of Solutré's site and those who lived here dates back to prehistoric times. The place known as the Crôt du Charnier, at the foot of the rock on what seems to have been an animals' migration route, is where the famous *Magma de Chevaux* (horse magma) was discovered. This is a gigantic pile made up of millions of bones of animals that were butchered and dismembered here 25,000 years ago. Flint worked into sharp, flat, laurel-leaf shapes and objects used by our distant ancestors in their daily lives were also found on the site. The region's Musée de Préhistoire (Prehistory Museum) at Crôt du Charnier itself exhibits a number of these artifacts. Opposite the rock, to the southeast, lie a string of villages composed of the humble homes of the *vignerons*. These all feature typical Mâcon cellars, constructed above or set into the ground of the steeply sloping streets.

In Solutré, the Romanesque church sits beside a communal washing place, surrounded by a covered gallery. The nearby hamlet of Pouilly has a small fifteenth-century château flanked by two round towers; Loché and Vinzelles both have Romanesque churches; and Fuissé is a charming, little market town. Like the whole of Burgundy, the villages of the Mâcon foothills felt the mark of the incredible expansion of Cluny Abbey, which lies not far from here on the other side of the mountains.

The Chardonnay kingdom

This area produces the Mâcon region's best wines, which, together with Chablis and the white wines of Côte de Beaune, complete the list of Burgundy's great white wines. The calcareous soils of the terroir, the hours of sunshine, and the favourable exposure to the sun are all instrumental in giving the wine produced from Chardonnay a marvellous personality. In a nutshell, the wine is a pale golden colour with green tints, a refined nose, and a lively, silky nature, with flavours of almond, hazelnut, acacia, and hawthorn heightened by a touch of minerals.

Pouilly-Fuissé – and the others…

Look to the southern vineyards of the vast Mâcon territory for the most remarkable wines. Pouilly-Fuissé is the most reputed and sought-after appellation and comes from Solutré-Pouilly, Fuissé, Chaintré, and Vergisson.

Wines from nearby Vinzelles and Loché may often be suppler and should be kept for a shorter time. They can be found under the Pouilly-Vinzelles or Pouilly-Loché ACs, or even the Mâcon-Villages AC.

Oingt

BEAUJOLAIS

Perched on top of a hill, the medieval village of Oignt reigns over the vast, vine-covered slopes.

Oingt stands out from other areas of Beaujolais because of its distinctive golden stone, after which the area is named. The beautiful, yellow-ochre limestone sparkles with tawny particles and gives the local architecture a characteristic golden colour. Part of southern Beaujolais, Oingt is located

within a large loop created by the Azergues Valley before the river of that name joins the Saône at Anse. Needless to say, different soils produce different wines, and those of Oingt leave the *crus* and Beaujolais-Villages wines produced in granite and schist soils far behind.

The heart of the golden land

Overlooking the Azergues Valley, Oingt is strategically located on the medieval frontier between Beaujolais and Lyon. The splendour of the medieval days is preserved in various relics, such as the sculptures of the great Oignt family situated below the vaulted arches of the choir in the fourteenth-century church. Not far from the "new château", this building is next to the site of old castle, whose remaining solid thirteenth-century tower has been converted into a panoramic viewing terrace.

Everywhere, there are remnants of the old fortified walls, from the Porte de Nizy gate to numerous historical dwellings, such as the Maison Commune. Below these houses, in the middle of the vines, stand two round turrets belonging to the Château de Prosny, built in the sixteenth century but frequently renovated since then. The hills and valleys of the area are covered in neat rows of Gamay grapevines. For a long time, because of the proximity to Lyon, the so-called "bastardized" Beaujolais of this golden-stone terroir was merely drunk as a thirst-quencher by the city's inhabitants.

Today, however, it has gained better credentials and is known for its lively, fresh personality, often accompanied by a delightful roundness that can take some time to develop. This uncomplicated wine is noticeably different from those produced in northern Beaujolais. `

Favourite Gamay territory

In 1395, Duke Philippe II le Hardi (The Bold) banned Gamay from the Burgundy soils that were little suited to it. Since then, it has become almost the exclusive variety of the granite and schist soils of Beaujolais and the calcareous clay soils of lower Beaujolais' golden stone region. There are numerous differences and styles among the various terroirs that cover a total of about 22,500 hectares, which is reflected in the ACs awarded here in the 1930s. Beaujolais is generally considered to be a fruity wine and comes mainly from the southern part of the region, which produces almost half of the yield. The remainder of the production is divided among the wines of the Beaujolais-Villages (6,000 hectares) from the best communes and the ten *crus* (6,900 hectares) from the truly elite plots, which bear the name of their village of origin on their labels. All share a delightful freshness and fruity flavour, but the best wines develop in depth and complexity and boast a refined personality with good definition.

Vaux-en-Beaujolais

BEAUJOLAIS

Vaux-en-Beaujolais, the village that most symbolizes Beaujolais, lies in the centre of this vast Gamay territory.

The village of Vaux-en-Beaujolais sits in the Vauxonne Valley, which runs through the region from west to east. This is the cultural centre of wine-growing Beaujolais and home to the headquarters of the Confrérie du Gosier Sec (Association of Dry Throats), whose members hold respected, traditional Bacchic celebrations every year. In 1934, Gabriel Chevalier of Lyons wrote a comic novel set here in Vaux-en-Beaujolais, called *Clochemerles*. Translated worldwide into thirty-three languages, the narrative describes the rhythm of life in a small Beaujolais village, which revolves around the events of the vine-growing and winemaking calendar, and relates comical and farcical everyday events.

Typically Beaujolais

Part of the Beaujolais-Villages appellation, the village of Vaux is set amid a sea of Gamay vines that cover the gently undulating hills descending from the foothills of the nearby mountains. The houses of the village are built around a charming Romanesque church and town hall. In the main square an interesting "squirrel" wine press is on display; the name derives from the method of powering the press – the village youths worked it in much the same way as a squirrel (or a hamster) turns the wheel of its cage.

The Musée de la Vigne et du Vin (Museum of Vines and Wines) tells the history of Beaujolais through the winemaking tools of the region. Visitors to Vaux will enjoy the quintessentially warm character of the people of Beaujolais. Their friendly hospitality is openly expressed and their innate good humour and cheeky, bawdy sense of well-being is reinforced with cups and goblets of Beaujolais wine, proffered along with pork aperitifs and local cheeses at every available opportunity.

Since the 1960s the arrival of the "Beaujolais Nouveau" wines has been celebrated here in Vaux in a typical festive atmosphere, and the event has now become something of a tradition. Beaujolais is famous worldwide for its pleasurable, thirst-quenching, lively, fruity wine.

Le Beaujolais Nouveau est arrivé!

Light, thirst-quenching, and pleasurable, Beaujolais is traditionally drunk from the beginning of winter, especially from the day of "St Cochon". This festival used to accompany – and sometimes still does – the annual slaughtering of pigs destined to become cured meats. The idea of turning the event into a large commercial event only dates back to the 1960s. Described as *nouveau* (new) – meaning of the same year – and *primeur*, which means in the first flush of youth, this wine is "liberated" from wine stores and cellars throughout the world on the third Thursday in November. Only the *crus*, which ideally "see Easter" before they are drunk, escape the early destiny of two-thirds of the Beaujolais production and one-third of that of the Beaujolais-Villages!

Arbois

JURA

The bell towers, mansions, and town houses of grand Arbois, surrounded by the Jura vineyards.

There is a long tradition of wine and trade in the foothills of the Juras, which face Burgundy's Côte d'Or. Vines grow in difficult conditions on the slopes facing west and southwest below Revermont, and further south on the slopes that cut quite deeply into the Jura's

Jura's specialities

In the Jura wine family, the Arbois appellation – 850 hectares – represents over half of the production. The white wine is mainly made from Chardonnay grapes, which are supplemented with varying proportions of Savagnin, a grape variety unique to the Jura. The red wines come mainly from two Jura varieties, Poulsard and Trousseau, with the addition of Pinot Noir. The Jura's great specialty, especially in Arbois, is the highly unusual *vin jaune*. Produced only by Vendanges Tardives (late harvest) of Savagnin grapes, this wine is left on its lees to mature in the barrel for at least six years and three months. It is not decanted

or topped up and evolves slowly under the protection of a veil of yeast that builds up on the surface. It acquires a complex and original character and a strong flavour reminiscent of walnuts and curry spices. Without an equivalent (except among fino sherries), it can be kept almost indefinitely in its special sixty-two-centilitre bottle, called a *clavelin*. Another specialty of the Jura is *vin de paille*, made from bunches of grapes dried on a bed of *paille* (straw) or suspended by a wire for two to three months. This produces a rich, sweet nectar, with powerful, candied fruit flavours.

limestone plateau. Like the surrounding countryside itself, the wines of Jura exhibit a great deal of individuality.

Strong personality

Arbois is located in the northern part of the Jura vineyards, at the mouth of the Planches Valley. The town is beautifully situated and nestles among clusters of vines next to the clear waters of the Cuisance River. Toughened by centuries of turbulence, the history of this proud town has alternated between prosperity and troubles.

The extensive remains of the thirteenth-century fortification walls include the Gloriette, Chaffin, and Prieuré towers and the round tower of Château Pécauld, whose bulky walls now house the Institut des Vins du Jura (Jura Wine Institute), the Musée de la Vigne et du Vin and the Porte Picardet. The Church of St Just is topped with a sixteenth-century bell tower, while the monasteries were founded a century later. The châteaux, such as the Château Bontemps which evokes days of favoured relations with the Dukes of Burgundy, and many of the old town houses are still in good condition.

In the centre of town is the Duchy of Burgundy's large cellar, known as Queen Jeanne's Cellar, which serves a reminder that this is essentially a wine town. In fact every house has its own cellar that opens onto the street by means of a small hatch. Villages near Arbois, notably Montigny-lès-Arsures or the hamlet of Pupillin, have similar buildings.

Arbois was home to Louis Pasteur, the scientist who studied wine fermentation and yeasts, and shed light onto the science of oenology. Today, the Maison Pasteur is a museum, and Pasteur's experimental vine, situated by the northern exit from Arbois on the road to Montigny-lès-Arsures, at a place known as En Rosières, is reverentially preserved and cared for.

Château-Chalon

JURA

Château-Chalon overlooks its vineyard, wholly planted with Savagnin, a grape variety unique to the Jura.

Typical of the Jura region, Château-Chalon is a village proudly stationed at the entrance to a hidden valley that intersects the edge of the limestone plateau. It opens out from vertical rocks above steep, southwest-facing slopes that are well-protected from the north wind and covered in vines. The plots cling dramatically to slopes that plunge down steeply from the village.

Down below, the Seille River flows from the Baume-les-Messieurs Circus around the base of the plateau.

A lofty site

Perched strategically high in an extraordinary location, Château-Chalon is a peaceful, aristocratic yet modest village. For nine or ten centuries it was home to a Benedictine abbey strictly reserved for women of noble birth, who brought fame to both Château-Chalon itself and to its wine. This abbey did not survive the French Revolution, but close by, the majestic Romanesque building of Baume-les-Moines Abbey (renamed Baume-les-Messieurs) still stands. Despite its more sheltered position at the back of the coomb where the Seille rises, it has been plundered over the years.

At Château-Chalon, only parts of the thirteenth-century château remain, along with the sixteenth- and seventeenth-century houses that were home to the canonesses. The Church of St Pierre displays a Romanesque bell tower, pointed Gothic vaulting in its nave, and a roof tiled with huge, flat, local limestone slates, called *laves*, that blend with the surrounding roofs.

Golden amber wine

The vineyards keep Château-Chalon's reputation alive, and today, wine is its most impressive monument. Once called *vin de garde* ("wine that keeps"), the wine keeps almost indefinitely, but it subsequently became famous as *vin jaune* ("yellow wine"), on account of its beautiful, golden amber colour. It has found a place in the world of wine somewhere between Hungarian Tokaji and Andalucian sherry.

The exclusive kingdom of vin jaune

A specialty of the Jura, *vin jaune,* is made by all the local appellations: Arbois, Étoile, and Côtes du Jura. But this highly unusual wine is the only wine to carry the Château-Chalon appellation. Other wines produced by the commune and nearby Domblans, Ménétru-le-Vignoble, and Nevy-sur-Seille, are classed as ordinary Côtes du Jura wine. Planted in marled clay soils, rich in small gravelly pebbles fallen from the cliffs, the rare Savagnin is the only grape variety authorized for the appellation's ninety hectares, of which only around fifty are cultivated today.

Production involves a small appellation area, slopes that are awkward to cultivate, small returns, and a lengthy and perilous gestation during which the initial volume is reduced by a third. The Château-Chalon AC is produced according to exceptionally strict rules. These include rigorous plot-by-plot inspection of the vines and the harvesting, with partial or total declassification as necessary, and authoritative tasting of the young *vin jaune,* which is repeated when the wine is put into the special sixty-two-centilitre bottles known as *clavelins.*

Cerdon

BUGEY

Bugey is a landscape of contrasts, from mountains, valleys, and forests, to rivers and streams. Cultivated vines grow in tightly packed, mosaic squares on the best plots of the sunny slope, next to forgotten vines that are now running wild. The stone *murgers* (walled enclosures) of the vineyards are overrun by scrub and dotted with small barns that have been abandoned. There are, in fact, only a few areas, notably on the right bank of the bend in the Rhône River, that carry on Bugey's viticultural tradition. And set just apart from these, near to the spot where the river Ain joins the Rhône, lie the unique vineyards of Cerdon.

Bugey's pearl

Cerdon is a living example of Bugey's traditional wine production. It is located behind the left bank of the Ain, in the hollow of a deep gorge on the Veyron River.

Nestled in the valley under the protection of its church, Cerdon keeps the region's wine-growing traditions alive.

The village is overlooked by steep hills, notably the "Grand Côte", dotted with small stone vineyard buildings, known here as *grangeons*. Streams tumble down between

Medium-dry sparkling rosé

Vin du Bugey Cerdon carries the *vin délmité de qualité supérieur* (VDQS) status and may, in homage to its originality, become one of the next appellations. It brings together the Gamay and Poulsard varieties from the nearby Beaujolais and Jura vineyards. Made into rosé, which is bottled before it has finished fermenting to imprison carbon gas bubbles and retain residual sugars, Cerdon is unique. This ancestral, natural method of production is different from that used by other sparkling wines and produces a delicately fruit-flavoured wine that is low in alcohol (around eight degrees) and slightly sweet. A simple drink that is pleasurable – and thirst-quenching!

the sturdy *vignerons'* houses with their wide, overhanging roofs and balconies. Numerous stone bridges and fountains add to the tranquillity of the village, which is calmly watched over by a church built halfway down the hill.

The breathtaking panoramic views from the surrounding heights, waterfalls, and caves all add to the unique charm of this area. The

villages of the appellation are also picturesque: Mérignat is a hilltop village perched below its feudal château; Poncin is a fortified medieval market town on the banks of the river Ain; Boyeux-St-Jérôme is in the upper part of the valley, alongside the hamlet of Châtillon-de-Cornelle, with a Gothic chapel belonging to the old château; St-Alban boasts a magnificent panoramic view; Bôches is an attractive wine-growing hamlet, and finally, Gravelles is a village (once better-known) on the opposite bank of the Ain. There are countless charming places to explore off the beaten track in this beautiful region. And, of course, another reason to linger here is to taste Cerdon's unique sparkling rosé wine.

Arbin

SAVOIE

Arbin, a small town gathered around its church, has become an important name in the Savoie vineyard.

From Arbin, the summit of Mont Blanc can be seen to the far northeast, while towards the south, the Belledonne mountain chain and the snowy peaks of the Maurienne Alps are visible.

Until the eighteenth century, Arbin lay under the shadow of the historical stronghold of Montmélian. Important traces of Montmélian's days as a medieval citadel have been left behind. It played a strategic role on this much-travelled route that was defended higher up the mountain by fortresses such as the Château de Cruet,

Deep, spicy Savoie Mondeuse

In antiquity, the reputation of the *coomb de Savoie* vineyard was mainly due to the Allobrogica vine, a variety mentioned by the ancient Roman scholar Pliny the Elder which seems to have played an essential role in vineyards from Savoie to the northern Côtes du Rhône around Vienne. This vine may have been the Mondeuse grape, a variety that bears comparison with Syrah. In any case, Arbin became the chosen terroir for the Savoie Mondeuse. The Vin de Savoie Arbin AC owes its character and its fame to this grape, which produces dense-coloured wines full of spiced fruit flavours that mature well, evolving to take on floral characteristics of violet and iris, with truffle nuances.

and by the Château de Miolans, down where the Isère River meets the Arc River. Since Roman times when a road was built through the Col du Petit-St-Bernard to link Italy to the Vienne and the Rhône rivers, wines from Savoie have benefited from good export routes and a solid reputation. Arbin, which only gained autonomy in 1779, was the keystone of Montmélian's vineyards.

Mountain-dwelling vignerons

Moulded to the southeastern flank of the Bauges range, the vineyards follow a string of

villages from Montmélian and Arbin to Fréterive, passing by Cruet, St-Jean-de-la-Porte and St-Pierre-d'Albigny. Tucked away at the foot of Thuile's mountain, the narrow streets of Arbin are dominated by the Church of St Nicolas, a reminder that Arbin once housed a Clunisien priory.

Lavish second-century mosaics have been discovered at the vast Gallo-Roman Mérande villa located on the road to Cruet near the sturdy main farm buildings of the Mérande – an old part of the feudal manor. Springs and fast-flowing streams are abundant here, but Arbin's watermills, which were so active in the past, are now derelict or have disappeared altogether. Only the vines continue the activities of the old days. Planted on slopes of limestone scree facing southeast, Jacquère is the dominant grape used for white wines, while Mondeuse produces unusual reds. These two local varieties distinguish the Savoy vineyard from those surrounding it.

Clambering up the foothills of Thuile, the Arbin vineyards face the Isère Valley and the distant Belledonne mountain chain.

Chignin

SAVOIE

The unique terroir of the steep slopes of Chignin are devoted to growing the Bergeron grape.

From Chambéry, the town of the "gatekeepers of the Alps" (the medieval Counts of Savoie who reigned over the Alps' main routes), the road follows a narrow valley leading southeast towards Montmélian and the right bank of the Isère. Sunlight is limited here as the valley is enclosed by the Bauges mountains to the north and the Chartreuse to the south – slopes that get the most sunshine have become small islands planted with vines. Opposite Aprémont and Abymes and overlooked by Granier's mountain, Chignin occupies a prime location at the foot of the southern slopes of the Bauges, facing due south.

Chignin-Bergeron

Chignin produces two of the seventeen local *crus* in a chain of Vin de Savoie appellations. The string of villages begins on the Upper Savoie side of Lac Léman, which is planted with the original Chasselas variety, borders the Rhône and the Lac du Bourget, and ends in the Isère Valley. Appellation Vin de Savoie Chignin is the classic preserve of the Savoie grape varieties, while the Vin de Savoie Chignin-Bergeron appellation is retained solely for the small Roussane grape production. From this exception, a rare (about 1,000 hectolitres) and highly desirable wine is born.

Village of towers

Chignin is a village of towers; at one time they numbered at least seven. Five of these towers remain, their ruins standing amid rows of vines that cover the hills before climbing up the lower slopes of the mountain to meet the woods.

With obscure origins that are probably medieval, the towers seem to mark out a fortified territory; they may have been used to watch over the valley and offer shelter if danger threatened. In the nineteenth century, the Tour de la Biguerne became part of a chapel dedicated to St Anthelme, who was born in the village. The other towers, left to the ivy and weeds,

remain silent sentries watching over Chignin, with its comparatively unpretentious eighteenth-century church tower. It is surrounded by charming hamlets: Tormery, overhung by a rock that was partly blasted away in 1913; Le Viviers; and Le Villard. Higher up the mountain, the Grotte de l'Ermite ("Hermit's Grotto") and the Trou ("Hole") de Chignin offer fantastic views over the whole area.

Bergeron, Prince of Chignin

Chignin's designated territory makes a vin de Savoie appellation *cru* that predominantly uses the Savoie grape varieties: Jacquère, which produces fresh, lively whites, and Mondeuse, which gives fleshy, perfumed red wines.

But, another Chignin mystery is the Roussanne grape variety, whose most favoured territory is the northern part of the Côtes du Rhône – namely Hermitage and St-Joseph. Known in Chignin under its ancient name of "Barbin", or its more common name of "Bergeron", the variety makes a perfect marriage with the terroir of these slopes: limestone scree extending as far as Francin and Montmélian. It produces one of the most beautiful, rare white Savoie wines, unctuous and elegant with flavours reminiscent of hawthorn, quince, apricot, and almond.

Chignin's grapes enjoy an unparalleled site, at the foot of the Bauges and opposite the Chartreuses.

Châteauneuf-du-Pape

RHONE VALLEY

When the popes took possession of the Comtat Venaissin territory and, from the beginning of the fifteenth century, chose to live in Avignon, they set their hearts on Châteauneuf and its vineyards; ever since, they've been considered "chosen by God". The pope's wine couldn't come from anywhere else, and as a result Châteauneuf's reputation rose to greatness. According to Baron le Roy, a pioneer of the AC at the start of the twentieth century, Châteauneuf is a "pontiff" at the heart of the vast Rhône Valley, whose wine "provides the fireworks at the conclusion of the great appellations of the Collines Rhodaniennes".

Châteauneuf, called "du Pape" ("of the Pope") since 1893, is positioned between the left bank of the Rhône and the Ouvèze. Blessed with an unrivalled terroir, the vineyards lie on an elevated plateau made mostly of shingle. The site enjoys optimal sunshine and the beneficial action of the mistral, the wind which chases the clouds and dries up the rain. It has all it needs to produce a prestigious vintage year after year.

Grown on harsh, pebble beds, Châteauneuf-du-Pape's vineyards were destined to produce wines of great character.

Where Grenache is king

As a way of preventing mediocrity and fraud, Châteauneuf-du-Pape pioneered the creation of ACs in the 1920s. Under the guidance of Baron Le Roy de Boiseaumarié, a lawyer and owner of Château Fortia, extremely strict production regulations were drawn up and a wide selection of grape varieties were decided – thirteen in total, a mixture of whites and reds, which, however, are very unevenly used today. Red, the predominant wine, makes up around ninety or ninety-five per cent of the production, depending on the year. Grenache is the favourite grape and may be the only variety used. However, it blends well with Syrah, Mourvèdre, and Cinsault, and sometimes with other, more minor varieties. The rarer white wines essentially use Grenache Blanc, Clairette, Roussanne, and Bourboulenc. This enables the creation of wines that possess quite diverse personalities, without losing – except in some modern experiments – their warm, fleshy character and rich, fruit-filled aromas. When added to aromatic plants and spices, these aromas evolve into a finish redolent of tobacco and truffles, with a gamey note: an enticing gastronomic invitation.

An exceptional destiny

Located between the Roman town of Orange and papal Avignon, Châteauneuf became the summer residence of the popes – among them, Clement V, the famous "Pape Clément" of the Bordeaux Graves region, and Jean XXII of Cahors, who built the castle and expanded the vineyard, assuring Châteauneuf a place in history.

The great Château des Papes was built in the fourteenth century, overlooking the village. All that remains of it today are the donjon (tower), a large stretch of wall, and a lower room, known as the "papal cellar", where the Echansonnerie des Papes (the local wine association) holds council. An enclosed vineyard serves as a reminder that this is where the local *vin de pays* forged its reputation.

The spectacular view takes in Avignon, the Dentelles de Montmirail cliffs, Mont Ventoux, and even the Alpilles (the foothills of the Alps). On the southern and eastern side, the small streets of the old village spread out in the shade of the bell tower of Notre-Dame-de-l'Assomption, a church with Romanesque origins that dates mainly from the eighteenth and nineteenth centuries. Elements of the eleventh- and fourteenth-century ramparts are still standing, as well as historical dwellings,

fountains and wells, oratories, and the tenth-century Chapel of St Théodoric. The past and the present are intertwined in the houses and wine cellars of the *vignerons*, bearing witness to the village's long-lived and unfailing wine trade.

Pebbles and vines

A sea of vines surrounds Châteauneuf, flooding over Courthézon and Bédarrides to the east, Sorgues to the south, and Orange to the north. The seabed of this viniferous ocean is pebbles. The whole plateaux is characterized by a base soil covered with large round pebbles, called *galets*, that have been rolled smooth by the Rhône. During the night, the stones release the heat accumulated in the daytime, providing superlative ripening conditions for the grapes. Although most lie on clay, some terroirs have a sandy soil, which conveys a special elegance to the wine. The combination of gradient, exposure, sunshine,

and the size of the pebbles determines the myriad terroirs that comprise over 120 localities, whose names have become those of the estates: La Nerthe, Fortia (or Fortiasse), Cabrières, Mont-Redon, La Gardine, Vaudieu, Le Rayas, etc.

At the centre of the large, highly regarded Crau lands in the southeastern part of the appellation lies an estate called the Vieux Télégraphe ("Old Telegraph"). This is the highest point in the area, where Claude Chappe, inventor of the semaphore, installed one of his communication systems at the end of the eighteenth century.

The châteaux of La Nerthe, Fortia, and Vaudieu are good examples of thirteenth-century architecture, while the Château des Fines Roches is an extraordinary nineteenth-century pastiche of a medieval castle.

Architecture and vineyards bear witness to the undiminished wealth and influence of "the castle of the popes" in all four corners of the region.

From its location on the left bank of the Rhône, the village of Châteauneuf-du-Pape lies under the protection of its castle, which commands a superb view of the surrounding countryside, as far as the distant Mont Ventoux *(overleaf)*.

Condrieu

RHONE VALLEY

Condrieu's crude terraces, which overlook the Rhône, are dedicated to growing Viognier, the local white grape variety.

Over the centuries, Condrieu acquired a reputation for being a village of *vignerons* and sailors. It's no wonder, considering its location perched high on the Piedmont of the Pilat Massif, on the edge of the Rhône River's right bank. Although river navigation is now a mere memory, having been supplanted by more modern forms of transport, the sailors played an active role in the history of Condrieu's golden era. They helped to spread the fame of the wines that have today brought prosperity to the northern Côtes du Rhône.

Château-Grillet, at the heart of Condrieu

Viognier is the famed grape variety that produces the only white Rhône appellation, Condrieu. But, there is also another area of production: a small enclave between Vérin and St-Michel-sur-Rhône, known by the name of this unique appellation's only property, Château-Grillet. The vines cover only around three hectares. They are marvellously situated around a sixteenth-century manor house, whose cellars date from an earlier building. The terraces create a small, well-sheltered amphitheatre, facing due south. Produced in secrecy, this wine is a legendary kind of Condrieu *grand cru*, both dry and unctuous, with flowery acacia, fruit, and light honey nuances.

Between the mountains and the Rhône

The village of Condrieu is situated on a wide bend in the Rhône that creates its territorial boundary. The vineyards tumble down to the river in a series of narrow, walled terraces that form sections of granite-based soil rich in mica – and therefore fairly unproductive.

At the end of the nineteenth century, the small returns from this incredibly difficult terrain worsened when the vines were ravaged by phylloxera. The vineyards were almost wiped out completely, and only started to come back to life in the 1970s.

The village has now regained the prosperity which, in former times, merited the building of the Tour du Garon and the great ramparts of the upper village, as well as the traditional houses of the lower area. The village church has a wonderful Romanesque interior that faithfully upholds the memory of its boatmen of old. Beside this stand the sumptuous sixteenth- and seventeenth-century Maison de la Gabelle and the Hôtel de Villars, two unmistakeable signs of Condrieu 's affluent history.

Viognier, the king

From Condrieu, the grape vines follow the banks and steep slopes of the ravines which have been cut into the hillside. The vines are exclusively Viognier, the only grape variety used in the *cru's* wonderfully aromatic white wine. The vineyards occupy the sunniest plots, both within the village and outside, in neighbouring Vérin, St-Michel-sur-Rhône, Chavanay, Malleval, St-Pierre-de-Bœuf, and Limony.

This sixteen-kilometre-long (ten-mile) ribbon of vineyards scarcely totals a hundred hectares (and even that is ten times larger than during the dark, postwar years), yet it produces the greatest white wine of the Rhône Valley. Called simply "Condrieu", this wine can be sweet and robust yet refined, with delicate violet, apricot, and almond nuances.

Gigondas

RHONE VALLEY

The simple pleasure of a small, shady square in the heart of Gigondas, in the hills of the Vaucluse.

The village of Gigondas is named after the Latin word *jocunditas*, meaning "joy" or "jubilation". But what exactly makes the inhabitants of this place so joyous? Is it the sheer beauty of the village's setting: up in the hills of the Vaucluse, just above the Ouvèze Valley where the Alps meet the Rhône Valley? Or could it be all the full-bodied wine produced here? The two are probably inseparable, in just the same way as the sloping hillsides that cling to the base of the

Dentelles de Montmirail cliffs characterize Gigondas' wine, which now stands beside Châteauneuf-du-Pape as a top Rhône red.

A special site, a unique character

Gigondas was for a considerable time a seigniory of the Principality of Orange, surrounded by land belonging to the Counts of Venaissin. It retains its fortified appearance from the past; the feudal castle with its Saracen tower, along with the protective ramparts, still seem to guarantee peace and security in the village.

The houses overlap one another around the Church of St Catherine, which features a small bell tower, and a sundial and clock that mark the slow passage of time.

Vines and olive trees have been cultivated here in Gigondas since ancient times; Roman legionaries, monks, and nuns have all farmed this land. However, the severe winter of 1956 completely destroyed the olive trees, ensuring the dominance of viticulture in the area ever since.

Beneath the vertical white cliffs of the Dentelles de Montmirail, a jagged landscape points skywards, covered in pines, oak trees, and broom. Below these, grape vines cover the slopes that tumble down towards the plain, extending beyond the village halfway down the hillside.

The land itself, its west-northwest exposure, and the southern French grape varieties that grow here all combine to produce the full-bodied, robust, and elegant wines of Gigondas. The long-lived wines demonstrate the personality that lies at the very heart of the Côtes du Rhône family of wines.

A great expression of Grenache

For a long time, Gigondas held a simple Côtes du Rhône classification, then it gained that of Côtes du Rhône-Villages; by 1971, the commune had obtained its own AC (guarantee of origin) status. Today, it covers 1,300 hectares distributed between the sluggish, sandy, calcareous soils in the upper vineyards (producing the more harmonious wines) and the ancient alluvial soils of the lower parts, which yield the warmer wines. Syrah and/or Mourvèdre and a few other varieties accompany Grenache, which is by far the principal grape. Rich, aromatic, and spicy, with pepper and liquorice nuances and low acidity, Grenache grapes benefit from a soil that is less warm than other Rhône Valley appellations, yielding wines with rare expression, freshness, and balance. These are the qualities that distinguishes it in the eyes of wine-lovers.

Old terraced houses (*right*) cluster on the hillside amid vineyards and olive trees under the Dentelles de Montmirail.

Grignan

RHONE VALLEY

Grouped on a rock in the middle of Coteaux du Tricastin, the houses of Grignan rise above the vines, with Mont Ventoux in the background.

The profuse letter writer, Madame de Sévigné, wrote of the enticing perfume that fills the village of Grignan. A seventeenth-century noblewoman, she spent much of her time in Paris, but her daughter was married to the Count de Grignan, so she made frequent visits here. In her spontaneous, quick writings, she praised the scent of aromatic plants, melons, figs, and Muscat grapes, but she complained of the region's rather harsh winters and the mistral that blew through the large rooms and corridors of the Château de Grignan.

Provence's Drôme region

Grignan lies in the heart of the Coteaux du Tricastin, which itself lies at the start of the southern Côtes du Rhône on the boundary

Balance and charm

The Coteaux du Tricastin attained AC status in 1973. Whether the ground is sandy earth or gravelly soil, the terroir has all the advantages of combining a northerly situation with a Mediterranean-influenced climate. The fresh-fruit flavours of the wine have a certain lively elegance and a delicacy that

distinguishes them from the Côtes du Rhône wines produced by their southerly neighbours. Although Grenache, Syrah, Cinsault, and Carignan are also the main grapes used, here Syrah is dominant, adding abundant fruit flavours with a touch of pepper that reinforces the personality of the red wines.

of the Dauphiné and Provence. The climate here is almost Mediterranean, and the grape vines grow beside lavender bushes, almond trees, and olive trees. Oak trees are also abundant and vital for the area's famous truffles.

The Château de Grignan stands on an outcrop above the village on the road to Valréas and St-Pantaléon-les-Vignes, its silhouette dominating the landscape. The château, a medieval stronghold transformed into a Renaissance residence that faces south towards the Midi, towers over the

mossy, grey-pink roof tiles of the village on the northern slope.

A belfry on top of the twelfth-century gates of Place de Sévigné watches over the streets that circle the foot of the hill. The terrace of the château sits above the collegiate Church of St Vincent, which marks the last resting place of Madame de Sévigné. From here, beautiful wide views stretch from the cliffs of the Dentelles de Montmirail and Mont Ventoux over to the Venaissin plain and the Alpilles, and

on the other side of the river Rhône, to the Vivarais Mountains.

Just a few kilometres away, the small village of Taulignan is particularly quaint, with small streets, tiny squares, and fountains all squeezed between its medieval fortification walls, complete with no fewer than eleven towers. From November to March, while the maturing Coteaux du Tricastin wine evolves its fruity flavours and spicy overtones, truffles take over the Sunday market at Taulignan and the Tuesday market at Grignan.

Château de Grignan dominates the village with its dramatic architecture and its sheer size.

Séguret

RHONE VALLEY

Rising among the Baronnies, the river Ouvèze joins the Rhône just after Sorgues. It flows across Vaison-la-Romaine and then travels diagonally south alongside the limestone hills and rocks at the foot of the Dentelles de Montmirail. The rugged cliff wall rises on its left bank, above the plain that once belonged to the Counts of Venaissin. This is where, guarded by the ruins of the feudal castle that overlook the valley, Séguret sits firmly on the rock. A delightful, picturesque village, Séguret dates from the infancy of Provence and has remained almost unchanged since the Middle Ages. The narrow, steeply sloping streets are *caladées* (cobbled) – a term used for the round cobblestones particular to the area. They wind among old houses built of warm-yellow limestone and lead to a surprisingly small square, home to the Mascarons fountain (where four grotesque

Winding cobbled streets and old houses with tiled roofs add to the charm of the village of Séguret.

faces spit out a stream of cool water) and the twelfth-century Church of St Denis.

Vines, olive trees, and orchards

In this delightful landscape, vines, olive trees, and orchards alternate on hillside terraces and gentle slopes. Like the whole Ouvèze Valley, Séguret has a long tradition of wine production, and today its wine has Côtes du Rhône-Villages status. Apart from the more reputed *crus*, these are the best Rhône wines. Perhaps because it is small in size, Séguret remains inconspicuous and is more inclined to peaceful village life than the tourist trail. Since 1960, it has combined its cooperative cellar with that of Roaix, another tranquil village situated on the right bank of the Ouvèze. It is a rare pleasure to visit these peaceful villages in their grand setting, and taste the wine on the spot.

Communal AC

The Côtes du Rhône-Villages Séguret is one of the commune appellations typical of the southern Rhône Valley. The Côtes du Rhône-Villages covers sixteen communes, half of which are located in the Vaucluse. Séguret produces mainly red wines, together with several rosés. Made from Grenache, Syrah, Cinsault, Mourvèdre, and several other smaller varieties, these wines are full-bodied and generous, with ripe fruit flavours and spicy notes. Like other wines from the Ouvèze Valley, these wines usually benefit from ageing, just like their big brothers, the Gigondas and Vacqueyras *crus*. More unusually, the white wines are notable for blends that can include Clairette, Grenache Blanc, Roussanne, Marsanne, and Bourboulenc.

Set in the magnificent hills that extend from the foot of the Dentelles de Montmirail (*below*), Séguret is one of the most beautiful villages of the area (*overleaf*).

Les Baux-de-Provence

PROVENCE

In a unique setting, Baux-de-Provence stands amid vines, olive, almond, and cypress trees.

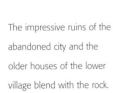

The impressive ruins of the abandoned city and the older houses of the lower village blend with the rock.

As the final barrier that faces the mistral before it reaches the Crau plain, the Camargue, and then the sea, the Alpilles foothills are subjected to a furious battering. Projecting between the Durance and the Rhône rivers, they are stocky but not particularly tall, forming a mixture of hills and jagged rocks. In the western part of the range, the citadel of Les Baux-de-Provence stands on a limestone spur – its name derived from *baou* in the old Provençal dialect, which also gave its name to the mineral Bauxite.

From its height, surrounded by vertiginous, sheer drops, the village overlooks the Val d'Enfer and the Fontaine Valley. The rock and the stone walls emerge together above the vines and the olive, almond, and cypress trees. The area is rich in bauxite, which takes its name from the village. This creamy white rock with reddish tints is high in iron oxide and alumina, and has been mined since the nineteenth century for making aluminium.

The "Provençal Acropolis"

The writer André Suarès aptly compared Les Baux with the Acropolis of ancient Greece, also built on a rock. Since the eleventh century, the citadel and its domain have maintained an

A charming village street (*left*) and the incredible, unique Provençal landscape (*right*) of Baux-de-Provence.

independent, even rebellious, stance under the auspices of the region's invincible rulers, the Barons or Seigneurs of Les Baux.

The village's unique aspect is striking. Erected on a summit, it appears to form a natural part of the rock, being half dug out of it and half built from it. The wild, spectacular ruins of the citadel form an enchanting, if chaotic aspect. Stretches of rock walls, steps, and stairways, and parts of towers and houses are dominated by a thirteenth-century tower overlooking the lower village on the western and southern slopes.

This lower part grew up during Baux's long integration into the old dominion of Provence,

and then into the kingdom of France. It has many noteworthy historical buildings, including grand fifteenth- and sixteenth-century houses such as the Hôtel de Manville, which is now the town hall and a museum, and the Hôtel des Porcelets, now a museum of works by the twentieth-century painter Yves-Brayer. Also of interest are the former chapel, now called the Santons (housing a collection of dolls) and lower down the Fontaine Valley, the Renaissance *casin* (small house) known as Queen Jeanne's Pavilion. The early Church of St Vincent has Romanesque additions, and the rustic Chapel of the Pénitents Blancs, which lies opposite, dates from the seventeenth century.

The omnipresent vine

The tidy village and its orderly rows of vines stand in stark contrast to the natural ravages wrought by erosion and the power of the mistral, as depicted in Van Gogh's paintings of Provence.

Vines were almost certainly present in the vast province of Narbonne, even before the Romans – who took over from the Massalians, colonizers from the city-state of Marseilles – cultivated them to make wine. The abundant archaeological evidence provided by the extensive Roman ruins at Glanum, on the road to St-Rémy-de-Provence, proves the extraordinary vitality of this area, which lay close to the Via Aurelia, the road which linked Arles to Rome in ancient times.

Along with the village of Baux, the appellation Les Baux-de-Provence is shared with the picturesque villages of St-Rémy-de-Provence, St-Étienne-du-Grès, Mouriès, Maussanne, Le Paradou, and Fontvieille. Located on the Arles road, Fontvieille is the village whose windmill was made famous by the writer Alphonse Daudet in his sentimental *Lettres de Mon Moulin*. He liked to visit here in order "to recover from the hectic pace of life in Paris", and the windmill now symbolizes the traditional way of life in rural Provence.

A recognized identity

For many years, Les Baux-de-Provence's vineyard came under the Coteaux d'Aix-en-Provence appellation, first as a VDQS, and then from 1985 as an AC. In 1995, the small western corner of this vast region was eventually awarded its own AC for red and rosé wines (the local olive oil also has its own appellation). The specific characteristics of the terroir are created from the arid, rocky ground, and a climate that is hot, dry, and windy, although better watered than that of the Coteaux d'Aix. The regulations of the Baux-de-Provence appellation are strict and employ high percentages of Grenache and Syrah, with the addition of Mourvèdre and a little Cabernet Sauvignon or Cinsault for the rosés. These warm, elegant wines develop a marvellous harmony after being laid down for several years and are definitely among the most desirable wines of Provence.

Bonnieux

PROVENCE

The houses of Bonnieux sit higgledy-piggledy around the church, on the edge of the Lubéron Massif (*right*).

The largest of several cliff-top villages, Bonnieux guards the northern entrance of the Lourmarin coomb – the short valley lying between the Petit Lubéron and the Grand Lubéron. The Aiguebrun River flows through the valley and the hills are covered with evergreen oaks. From its coveted location on a promontory in the Petit Lubéron, Bonnieux has had to face numerous enemies throughout history.

Neolithic man settled here, and the countryside is scattered with innumerable *bories*: small, primitive, dry-stone buildings. The incredible Pont Julien dates back to the first century BC and bore traffic throughout the Roman era. The bridge stands on the Via Domitia – the Roman road of Provence – and crosses the river Calavon.

Meanwhile, the position of the Catholic village of Bonnieux directly opposite that of Protestant Lacoste – where the ghost of the Marquis de Sade allegedly still haunts the château – brings back memories of an often bloody past.

A cliff-top village

Bonnieux overlooks the Calavon Valley and the countryside around Apt, known for its ochre-coloured earth. The village hugs a pyramid-shaped, rocky outcrop, the outline of which forms a dramatic backdrop to the statue of the Virgin surmounting the spire of the church's bell tower. This part-Romanesque, part-Gothic church is roofed with flat, round stones. It dominates the surrounding area, and from its terrace there is a panoramic view over Lacoste, Gordes, Roussillon, and far in the distance, Mont Ventoux.

Among the ruins of the thirteenth- to fifteenth-century ramparts, the steep streets are the same pale honey-colour as the local stone. Old houses and town houses, such as the Hôtel de Rouville (now the town hall), indicate the wealthy past of this village that was once a fortified papal town and part of Provence's Comtat Venaissin.

Between the fortified towns and villages, vines add a garland to the splendours of the Parc Naturel du Lubéron, a national park and nature reserve. Throughout the ages, the vineyards have been an integral part of this rich countryside.

The newborn Côtes du Lubéron

For a long time, the Lubéron vineyard was restricted to producing dessert grapes. It has now rediscovered a viticultural tradition that, in 1988, earned it the Côtes du Lubéron appellation. The zone is situated between Apt and Cavaillon, and comprises thirty-six villages, all contained within the Parc. Covering 3,400 hectares, the vineyard's sandy, crumbling limestone soils suit the traditional Rhône Valley grape varieties. Grenache and Syrah dominate the compact red wines, which are distinguished by red- and black-fruit flavours with woody, mushroom undertones. These same southern varieties benefit from cool nights, which prolong ripening and bring forth marvellously expressive rosés, with delicate, elegant fruit flavours. The white wines are worthy of note. Blending Grenache Blanc, Ugni Blanc, Clairette, Bourboulenc, Rolle, and Roussanne, they marry a combination of floral and fruity notes with grace and elegance.

The vines that cover the slopes opposite Bonnieux come under the Côtes du Lubéron appellation.

Brignoles

PROVENCE

The small streets, squares, and fountains of the Var region add to the delightful tranquillity of the villages.

The Côte d'Azur, with its busy beaches and the bustle of tourists, seems miles away. Inland, the Var opens out into a landscape of hills, valleys, and delightful rural villages surrounded by vineyards and olive groves and the cool shade of juniper trees, oaks, and pines. Here and there, earth coloured red by iron bauxite surfaces amid the rich vegetation that is nourished by the southern sunshine.

Flowing down from the eastern slopes of the Ste-Baume Massif, the river Caramy passes below the small Merovingian Gayole Chapel which is enclosed by rows of vines. It continues past the impressive Romanesque La Celle Abbey – which today houses a wine museum, the Maison des Vins des Coteaux Varois – before running around the base of Brignoles, an old market town used as a summer residence by the Counts of Provence. The small river then joins the Argens, just before Thoronet Abbey. This building was a masterpiece of Provençal Romanesque architecture, and its austere, plundered ruins stand in stark contrast to the wild, natural landscape.

At the heart of the Var region

Brignoles sits on a hill, right at the centre of the Var vineyards. Its old, narrow streets lead towards the Palace of the Counts of Provence. Today, the local Musée du Pays Brignolais occupies the attractive thirteenth-century building and its sixteenth-century chapel. Inside, the most interesting exhibit is a third-century sarcophagus originally from the Gayole Chapel, which is probably the earliest monument to the Christian Gaul era in France.

St-Sauveur is a typical Provençal combination of a church and a market in one building, with a large Gothic nave and a Romanesque doorway. The spire rises high above the tiled roofs of the village. Numerous old houses have survived, and there are remnants of ramparts, towers and entrance gates, such as those of St-François and St-Pierre, which used to display a *vierge noire* (black Virgin statuette), now in the museum.

The slopes and *restanques* (narrow terraces) of this part of Provence are devoted to the large family of Provençal grape varieties that were given a new lease of life when the Coteaux Varois AC was established in 1993. Twenty-seven other villages around Brignoles all add a variety of nuances to the wines of the AC. By combining grapes grown under a maritime influence with those of a higher altitude on the *côtes*, Provençal producers have managed to create wines that are known for being especially fresh.

La Celle Abbey – jewel of the Coteaux Varois

La Celle's royal abbey is one of the most beautiful Romanesque treasures of the Var. Built in the eleventh century, it was a famous convent, but by the seventeenth century had acquired such a scandalous reputation that it was dissolved. Now restored, it belongs to the Conseil Général du Var (the regional authority) and houses the Maison des Vins des Coteaux Varois. Apart from the objects and tools associated with the production of wine, the Maison hosts a variety of activities, such as wine exhibitions and tastings. In the grounds, a walled conservation vineyard displays an extensive collection of eighty-eight Provençal grapes, including even the rarest varieties. The cultivation of grapes in the Coteaux Varois AC is studied in the enchanting, symbolic, and historical setting of the abbey estate, which features a model vineyard and a research vineyard.

The former summer
residence of the Counts of
Provence now houses the
Musée du Pays Brignolais.

Cassis

PROVENCE

The steep slopes of Cassis's deep, limestone bay (*overleaf*) are home to terraced vineyards.

"**B**row facing full south, feet in the sea", wrote Provençal poet Frédéric Mistral of Cassis. No one could have described it better – but then, inspiration does come easily in this beautiful place.

Phoenician Greeks chose to settle Cassis, a harbour on the shores of the Mediterranean Sea, on account of its natural advantages. Today, ochre-coloured houses line the back of the inlet, which is surrounded by hills and rocky ridges and dwarfed by Cap Canaille, a tall white cliff with russet tones that rises 400 metres (1,312 feet) above the sea. The

A maritime wine

Cassis is a small AC covering 180 hectares, with a characteristic limestone terroir laid out on wide terraces that stretch all the way to the sea. Three-quarters of the vines are reserved for the production of *blanc de blancs*, the most famous of Cassis' wines. Made from white varieties such as Clairette, Marsanne, Ugni Blanc, Bourboulenc (known here as Doucillon), and Sauvignon, this wine is full of aromatic nuances and possesses a personality that is essentially maritime in origin. The warm, pleasant red and rosé wines are produced from Grenache, Cinsault, and Mourvèdre.

small fishing port – now a summer haven for tourists – and the surrounding *calanques* (mini fjords) mirror the shimmering sunlight that inspired Impressionist painters such as Paul Signac, who is best-known for painting this place.

A rare, natural site

The *coteaux* are made up of wide, terraced strips of land on the slopes of the hills and at the foot of Cap Canaille, where rows of vines run through clusters of pine and olive trees. This natural

amphitheatre reduces the violence of the mistral to a gentle breeze, and the humidity of the sea combines with an exceptionally sunny situation.

It is hardly surprising, therefore, that the viticultural potential of this site attracted the attentions of eleventh-century canons from Marseille, the fourteenth-century king René and sixteenth-century Florentine nobles. Nor that at the beginning of the twentieth century, when the vineyards of France were recovering from the damage caused by phylloxera, the *vignerons* of Cassis

were among the first to champion the concept of the *appellations d'origine* – along with those of Arbois and Châteauneuf-du-Pape – to protect their terroir and its unique identity.

Provence mainly produces rosé, but Cassis is dominated by the production of a characterful white wine, in which Frédéric Mistral detected "the aroma of rosemary, heather, and myrtle". It is an excellent companion for seafood dishes and local specialties such as *bouillabaisse*, *anchoïade*, and *aïoli*, as well as for simple fish, such as sea bass or *rascasse*.

In the port of Cassis, small fishing boats and brightly coloured houses glow in the Mediterranean sunlight.

Ménerbes

PROVENCE

Nostradamus, the sixteenth century author and seer, called Ménerbes "a stone ship in the midst of a sea of vines". His metaphor is still the best description of the village. From the top of its promontory, with the Lubéron behind it, Ménerbes surveys the plain extending northward as far as the Vaucluse Mountains. The silhouette of Mont Ventoux is visible on the distant horizon. During the turbulent sixteenth century, the time of the Religious Wars, this village was an almost unassailable stronghold which only surrendered after a long siege.

A fortified village

Moulded into the shape of the rock, the medieval ramparts support buildings on the edge of the escarpment. They run east to west, from the "bow" to the "stern" of the metaphorical ship, above the trees and terraces that descend the slopes step by step. In the "bow", the thirteenth-century citadel has been damaged and restored several times. In the "stern", the simple, charming fourteenth-century church with its terraced graveyard offers wonderfully wide, peaceful views over the surrounding countryside. Down below,

With narrow streets climbing up to the summit (right) and fortifications all around (far right), Ménerbes is one of the most picturesque villages of the Côtes du Lubéron (overleaf).

the *castellet* (tiny castle), a medieval and Renaissance building endowed with two huge towers, provides an advance defensive position.

At the centre of the village, sixteenth- and eighteenth-century houses and large dwellings are built next to one another around sheltered, almost secret, private gardens. The belfry of the old town hall rises up to the heavens, topped by a fine, seventeenth-centur, forged-iron campanile that is characteristic of a countryside constantly subjected to the fierce assaults of the mistral.

An old tradition, a young appellation

Under the sun's playful rays, the blue of the sky contrasts with the colours of the crops and the earth. This intense blue is found in the work of Nicolas de Staël, many of whose paintings were made in the *castellet*'s studio at Ménerbes.

All around the village, orderly rows of vines, softened by the curving landscape, form battalions of southern grape varieties – Grenache, Syrah, Clairette, and several others – under the authority of the citadel. Underestimated for a considerable time despite the long history of the local viticultural tradition, the Côtes du Lubéron won the battle to gain an AC in 1988 and has today joined the ranks of the great Provençal Rhône Valley appellations.

The Corkscrew Museum

Naturally enough, the Citadelle Estate in Ménerbes has built its reputation on Côtes du Lubéron wine, but it is also known for the Musée du Tire-Bouchon, which is housed in one part of this marvellous dwelling and brings together more than a thousand corkscrews from different countries in the world. From its first appearance in the seventeenth century, after the cork and bottle were developed, the corkscrew was a luxury object and remained so until bottling became common practice. Made of wood, bronze, gold or silver, and steel, corkscrews were decorated in many ways and incorporated all manner of technical sophistications – operating with double screws, cogs, levers, etc. A great deal of ingenuity went into their design. Nothing was too good for the key that unlocks a world where dreams are made.

St-Roman-de-Bellet

NICE

Vineyards cover the *restanques* (terraces) of the northwestern hills of Nice in the appellation of Bellet.

Surprisingly, the hamlet of St-Roman-de-Bellet and the small AC vineyard of Bellet are an integral part of Nice. This large city is famous for the Bay of Angels, the Promenade des Anglais, the flower market of the old town, Roman ruins at Cimiez, Baroque religious buildings, small village streets and cosmopolitan splendour, the Carnival and Niçoise cuisine. Its extensive territory, however, overlaps the foothills of the Préalpes, which are slowly being conquered by the urban demands of this capital of the Côte d'Azur.

Vineyard in the city

Until the arrival of the railway, the city was restricted to the confines of what is today called Old Nice. Even in those days, however, it owned a large vineyard on hillsides northwest of the centre, above the left bank of the Var, near St-Roman-de-Bellet. However, at the end of the nineteenth century, an area totalling over 1,000 hectares was reduced to almost nothing by phylloxera.

The vineyard was resurrected nonetheless, and in 1941 was granted an AC on account of its past reputation. It is gaining hectare after hectare despite fierce competition from market gardeners and carnation growers, both of whom are fighting developers over terraces wanted for villas and housing. And it must be said that these are prime building sites! Vines only cover fifty of the 650 hectares designated by the appellation zone.

St-Roman-de-Bellet is a small *Nissart* (of Nice) hamlet with rural charms, including a wonderful location, châteaux, and wine-producing domains. These are scattered alongside its *restanques* (terraced hillsides), dotted with olive and eucalyptus trees. Incredibly sunny, the terraces are refreshed by the cool winds that blow from the mountains in the morning and those that blow off the sea in the evening. The views are stunning, overlooking the Alps and the Var Valley. And the wine, livelier than its southern associates, retains the special flavour of the Provençal sun, allied to the nearby sea and the neighbouring mountain.

Unusual varieties

Apart from its urban site, the Bellet vineyard is also unusual because it is planted almost entirely with local grape varieties. The red wine blends the rich and refined Braquet, which is often the dominant variety in the rosés, with Folle Noire, an aromatic, colourful but capricious grape. These two may be finished with Grenache and Cinsault.

Rolle, a white grape of the Italian Vermentino family, grows well here and is sometimes mixed with Chardonnay, which is not really a Provençal variety. Different from other wines of Provence, the red, white, and rosé of Bellet are crisp and light. They demonstrate a particular stylistic elegance and a harmonious union of aromas.

The hills of St-Roman-de-Bellet boast vines, woods, and beautiful houses, such as the Château de Bellet (*overleaf*).

Patrimonio

CORSICA

Patrimonio lies between the sea and the mountains, where the vast Nebbio territory forms a natural amphitheatre opening towards the west and lower parts of Cap Corse. Its pace of life is governed by the rhythms of the vine – a far cry from the bustle of the tourist port of St-Florent, which is actually only a few kilometres away. The land here is undoubtedly rich and has been coveted through the centuries by many invaders, especially the Genoese, who wanted it not only to acquire strategic positions in the Mediterranean, but also for its vineyards, olive and chestnut groves, and flourishing orchards.

The Conca d'Oro

This land here is so rich that it is called the Conca d'Oro: the "golden conch". It overlooks the bay that shelters the town and port of St-Florent, where the somewhat feeble waters of the river Poggio join those of the Alisio, to be only barely strengthened by the Guadello.

Positioned over the water, St-Florent boasts a Genoese citadel and the wonderful Nebbio Cathedral, a Romanesque building delicately sculpted out of the pale-yellow limestone that is the pride of the surrounding area.

Patrimonio's vines are planted in the foothills of the mountain that culminates at the Col de Teghime – a fantastic viewpoint overlooking the east and west coasts as well as the Serra di Pigno,

The vineyard at the end of the Ile de Beauté

In 1968, Patrimonio became the first Corsican AC, and its *vignerons* declared their intention to renew the vineyards, which were replanted with the best traditional grape varieties from the 1980s. On Patrimonio's chalky clay soils, Nielluccio, twin brother to the Tuscan Sangiovese grape, is unrivalled among the reds. Strong, firm, velvety tannins with good acidity ensure that its wines are full of spice and elegance, are well-balanced and can be laid down. Vermeille – here called the Malvoisie Corse – endows the white wines' incredible aromatic finesse with nuances of ripe fruits and white flowers. And also, under the label of Muscat du Cap Corse, the Muscat variety "with small grapes" creates a white *vin doux naturel*: a fortified sweet wine that is mellow and unctuous, with intense aromas – bursting with sunshine.

before falling back down to Bastia. The vines cover the slopes and hills that mould the landscape right down to the sea.

Halfway up the mountain, the first sight of the unpretentious village of Patrimonio is of the sixteenth-century Church of St Martin. The rough, unfinished appearance of its tall, nineteenth-century

bell tower, a strong, attractive construction with regular holes that once held the scaffolding, is in keeping with the rugged, mountainous rock.

In the shadow of the church stands U Nativu, a late megalithic, anthropomorphic menhir (upright statue) dating from the eighth to ninth century BC, a reminder of the island's ancient history.

On the foothills of Mont Sant'Angelo, rows of Nielluccio and Malvoisie grapes clamber toward the neighbouring towns of Poggio d'Oletta and d'Oletta. Lower down, the vines run alongside limestone rocks eroded in extraordinary formations before, refreshed by the spray and the sea air, they touch the sand on the Farinole shores.

Patrimonio sits at the foot of the mountain, behind the Golfe de St-Florent, overlooking its vineyard.

Lagrasse

LANGUEDOC

An abbey on the edge of the Orbieu

Making its way from the heart of the Corbières Mountains across narrow gorges, steep ridges, and river basins covered with vineyards, the river Orbieu skirts the Montagne d'Alaric before flowing through Lagrasse and on to join the Aude near Narbonne. Situated where the river Alsou meets the Orbieu, Lagrasse boasts a strategic location.

The village grew up on the right bank of the river in a natural amphitheatre created by the surrounding mountains. Halfway up the slopes, vines and olive trees give way to the *garrigue* scrub and woodland of the upper heights.

On the opposite bank, over the Pont Vieux, stands the enormous Benedictine Ste-Marie-d'Orbieu Abbey, to which this place has owed almost everything since Carolingian times. Here, all styles and periods are recorded in stone, from the pre-Romanesque tenth-century tower to the eighteenth-century cloister. The abbey church, chapel, old palace, thirteenth-century monastery dormitory, monumental fourteenth-century tower and bell tower, and eighteenth-century new palace form a remarkable collection of buildings.

Lagrasse was formerly huddled within the oval enclosure of the ramparts, whose remains include the twelfth-century Tour de Plaisance and the fourteenth-century Porte de l'Eau ("Water Gate"). The medieval village retains a network of narrow streets and squares with old houses – the Maison Maynard, the Maison Lautier, the Maison Sibra, and the presbytery that is now the Maison du Patrimoine – all overlooked by the impressive bell tower of the Gothic church of St Michel.

Lagrasse means "fertile" in the old French Occitan language. Today the village focuses on making wine, being one of eleven communes in the huge Corbières appellation. Everything is favourable for growing grapes here, from the Mediterranean climate refreshed by the altitude to the protection of the Montagne d'Alaric against the fierce "Cers" wind and the red soils on limestone. Each imprints the wines with a unique identity.

Amid vines and olive trees on the banks of the Orbieu, the village of Lagrasse is charged with history.

The Montagne d'Alaric, between Carcassonne and Narbonne, is more than just an exceptional natural orchid reserve. Situated at the gates of the Cathar country, the region also has a rich and rather turbulent patrimonial history, both military and religious. The fortified villages, châteaux, and abbeys surrounding the rocky massif seem to suit the landscape's rough grandeur. In contrast, the rows of vines offer a civilized influence. Along with the olive trees, these vines have never failed the area, be it the Narbonne province of Gallo-Roman times or the Aude *département* of today.

The terroir of Corbières

The main trump in the Corbières AC pack is the diversity of its grape varieties. These mainly comprise the following: Carignan, Grenache, Syrah, Mourvèdre, and Cinsault for the reds; Grenache Blanc, Maccabeu, Bourboulenc, Clairette, Marsanne, Roussanne, and Muscat for the whites. Such a wealth of choice permits great freedom of expression, depending on the terroir. In the Lagrasse area, where the grapes benefit from a Mediterranean climate as well as a long, late ripening period, the wines are fleshy, well-balanced, and intensely aromatic, with a nose of fruits scented with the herb flavours of the *garrigue*.

Lagrasse's past may be seen all around, from its narrow streets and beautiful old houses (*left*), to the oval structure in the shape of the old ramparts (*overleaf*).

Minerve

LANGUEDOC

Minerve, the emblem of the Minervois appellation, sits proudly on its rocky promontory surrounded by sheer drops.

For a long time, Minerve was isolated on its rock in the peninsula where the river Cesse meets the river Brian. This area is home to the last foothills of the Cevennes and makes an impressive landscape, with grottoes and gorges carved out of the limestone plateau that show white amid the *garrigue* scrub, the kermes oaks (an evergreen species), and the juniper trees.

Minerve is a true *roc-ciutat* ("rock city"), built on a rocky peninsula, surrounded by the vertical sides of ravines gouged out by the two rivers. It is linked to the plateau by a narrow passage which was closed off in the Middle Ages, when the château of Minerve added fortifications. These didn't prevent fanatical crusader Simon de Montfort from capturing the village in 1210, however, in an attempt to wipe out supporters of

Catharism, a belief structure considered heretical by the Catholic Church. He cut off the Cathars' water supply and after a long siege, burned 140 of the "Perfects", or Cathar elders, at the stake.

Minerve, symbol of Minervois

Today, the village is no longer isolated. Linked to the west bank by a nineteenth-century stone bridge built forty metres (131 feet) above the Cesse, Minerve draws many visitors and wine enthusiasts.

The old Cathar citadel has retained its medieval appearance and former dignity. After various attempts at demolition, there is almost

The extensive and diverse Minervois AC

The Minervois wine-producing area, a huge, south-facing natural amphitheatre that backs onto the side of the Montagne Noire, extends into the Hérault and Aude *départements*. This offers the AC a range of different styles of terroirs planted with a mixture of old and more recent Languedoc varieties such as Grenache, Carignan, Syrah, and Mourvèdre. Apart from the differences due to the terroir, its red wines are dense, warm, and vigorous. And on the limestone plateau above Cesse, around St-Jean-de-Minervois, Muscat grapes produce a *vin doux naturel* that is especially fine and delicate.

nothing left of the thirteenth-century château, apart from a great octagonal pillar known as the Candela that rises up out of the ruins. Remains of the double defense system are visible in many parts of the village: its rampart walkway; towers – the tower known as Tour de la Prison; and its gates – the thirteenth-century Porte des Templiers (Templars Gate). All still seem to stands guard over the old, limestone houses.

On a slightly higher level, the simple rustic charm of the Romanesque Church of St-Étienne remains unaltered since Cathar times. Below the ramparts over the Brian River and accessed by a covered pathway, the St Rustique well may be found – the very well that was blocked by the crusaders to deprive Minerve of water.

The most unusual monument in Minerve is probably the river Cesse itself. It is bridged by two natural rock formations called the Pont Grand and the Pont Petit through which the water surges after storms and heavy rain.

The vineyards that cover the nearby slopes of the village have given their name to the whole Minervois region, a huge stretch of terraces and hillsides. And as well as the name, of course, Minerve offers its proud and wild personality.

In a spectacular setting deep in the Minervois, the Cathar stronghold retains its rustic medieval appearance.

Roquebrun

LANGUEDOC

On the banks of the Orb and the mountainside, Roquebrun's microclimate is ideal for viticulture.

The Orb, a small river, is aptly named after the round curves and loops it makes on its way down through the foothills of Larzac toward Béziers and the Mediterranean Sea. From the foot of the Monts de l'Espinouse, it alters direction to flow directly south, carving out a passage through the towering gorges. Further on, the river meanders along in great curves, and provides Roquebrun with a wonderful site for growing grapes.

A terroir of schist

the Coteaux du Languedoc has fourteen *crus*; three of them – Faugères, Clairette du Languedoc, and St-Chinian – have individual appellations. The latter comprises 2,100 hectares and twenty villages which share two different kinds of soils: schist in the northern part and chalky clay soils in the south. The most characteristic wines of the AC come from grapes grown on schist slopes. Like the neighbouring village of Berlou, Roquebrun has distinguished itself by gaining the right to add the village's name to the St-Chinian appellation since 2004. Perhaps this may be the first step towards gaining its own AC. Grown on fairly poor soil, Grenache, Carignan, Syrah, Mourvèdre, and Cinsault develop complexity and finesse, producing firm, velvety tannins, which make wines that should keep for some time. Carignan is becoming less popular in the face of Syrah's recent rise in favour, and Grenache gives an intense burst of flavour reminiscent of certain traditional *vins doux naturels*, characterized by aged *rancio* nuances.

Built on a rocky slope that overhangs the right bank, the village enjoys an extraordinarily well-sheltered location, as evidenced by the abundant orange and mimosa trees, and the exotic plants in this charming "Mediterranean garden".

The Hérault's "little Nice"

Formed around a peak that is still guarded by the tower of the old Carolingian castle, the village has progressively expanded down towards the river and along the left bank. The most fertile and easily tamed lands have been cultivated. As well

as grape vines, cereal crops and olive trees have brought prosperity to the village, as is evident from the old mills on the edge of the Orb that were used for making flour and olive oil.

The microclimate that has given Roquebrun its nickname of "the little Nice of the Hérault" defines one of the most remarkable terroirs of the St-Chinian appellation. It is especially favourable for growing vines, which fight for space on the best slopes with small evergreen oaks called kermes, strawberry trees (*arbutus*), rock roses (*cistus*), and heathers.

The steep and fairly unproductive slopes are mainly composed of schist: the brown-coloured rock that gives a particularly rustic character to the Laurenque hamlet above Roquebrun. From both the schist and the hot, dry climate, the Languedoc grapes derive a character which combines ripe fruit flavours with the minerals of the terroir. They produce wines that are dense yet quite fine, with one of the strongest personalities of all the St-Chinian wines and, on a wider scale, of the entire Languedoc region.

Southern grape varieties thrive by the edges of the Orb and on the surrounding schist hillsides and slopes.

Banyuls

ROUSSILLON

The mountains of the Albères are found in this, the most southerly part of the French vineyard (with the exception of Corsica in the middle of the Mediterranean). Just a few hundred yards from the Spanish border and the Costa Brava, this region only became part of France in the seventeenth century.

Here, the rugged rocks form a protective enclosure for the hillsides, creeks, and beaches of the Côte Vermeille. In the western distance stands the silhouette of Canigou, the legendary Pyrenean mountain, while Collioure and Port-Vendres to the north and Cerbère to the south frame the village.

Emphasized by headlands that extend towards the sea, this rugged, rocky shoreline, shared with olive trees and wasteland, seems the most astonishing terroir for growing grapes. Yet, Banyuls is the name of the extraordinarily special *vins doux naturels* (fortified dessert wines) that are produced here. The red wines and rosés are left to Collioure.

Perilous terraces

Banyuls is located at the mouth of the Baillaury and its small prosperous valley. Puig del Mas, set slightly further back in the hillside above the river's right bank, was of equal importance during the Middle Ages, and concerned itself with producing wine while Banyuls concentrated on fishing. Though

Vin doux naturel, Banyuls' specialty, is sometimes aged in barrels left out in the sun to strengthen its strong, powerful character.

The ultimate Grenache

The Banyuls AC represents the ultimate extreme that Grenache can attain in a purely Mediterranean style, with its *vin doux naturel*. The tradition derives from harvesting overripe grapes and an original method of winemaking that was refined during the thirteenth century. Alcohol is added to the must of fermenting grapes to stop fermentation at a certain point, thus retaining some of the wine's natural sugar. The perfect balance between alcohol and residual sugar creates rich, powerful wines with velvety tannins which ensure that they can be kept for a long time, either in tuns (small barrels) – where they may gain *rancio* notes – or after early bottling, when they are known as *rimages* vintages.

much reduced today, you can still see the occasional fishing barges drawn up on the stony beaches.

Vines growing on the very first slopes form the backdrop to the various quarters of the old town surrounding the creek: the Rectorie quarter, which with its Romanesque church surrounded by cypress trees, is more impressive than the twentieth-century church at Banyuls; the colourful, picturesque Pointe d'Houme quarter, and the Ile Grosse. Linked to the port by the pier, this island offers magnificent views of the coastline, while the nineteenth-century Chapel of Notre-Dame-de-la-Salette, built 200 metres (656 feet) above sea level, has a fantastic panoramic viewpoint.

The vineyards are scattered with *casots* – small dry-stone refuges built to shelter the *vigneron* and his tools. Made of narrow terraces whose low walls tame the gradients and whose furrows drain off excess water, these vineyards have created extraordinary oblique networks, ridged like *peus de gall*, the dialectical term for "cockerel's feet".

It is extremely difficult to cultivate vines here. Harvesting can only be done by hand and the earth has to be replaced when storms devastate the slopes. Such extreme conditions, combined with the sun, the Tramontagne (wind that blows off the mountain), and the sea air, leave their mark on the wine, whose "bearing and Saracen warmth" were praised by the French gastronome Curnonsky (Maurice Edmond Sailland).

On the steep slopes around Banyuls (*overleaf*), wine-growing is rough work, but it is rewarded at the end of harvest with traditional Catalan celebrations (*above*).

Collioure

ROUSSILLON

The wild beauty of the Côte Vermeille – barely tamed by the tourist trade of the seaside – was made for painters who work in pure colour. Thus it was an ideal setting for the Fauves group of artists, who painted here at the beginning of the twentieth century. Dusky purplish-pink schist and many-toned grey limestone contrast with the intense blues of the sea and the sky.

On the eastern extremities of the Pyrenees, the tattered, rocky spikes of the Albères descend abruptly into the Mediterranean, dividing the shoreline into a series of creeks, coves, capes, promontories, and deep valleys.

The winds and sea air play a primordial role in the unusually hot, dry climate, and while Catalan boats gleam in the sunshine that penetrates the port, the vines of the sometimes vertiginous hillsides bask in its rays. These slopes were destined to become one of the highlights of Mediterranean viticulture.

Catalan jewel

The small Catalan port of Collioure is open to all maritime trade routes. Occupying one of the sheltered creeks on the coast, it belongs to the same appellation zone as neighbouring Port-Vendres and Banyuls. The Route des Crêtes, which winds in and out of the Albères foothills, provides scenic views as it runs by the Notre-Dame de la Consolation Hermitage and the Tour de Madeloc. This signal tower – a large, round,

schist lookout post – has surveyed the vast
expanse of sea since the thirteenth century.
On the coast, beaches and rocky promontories
delineate Collioure's remarkable setting. The
Church of Notre-Dame des Anges, which is built
over the sea, is a seventeenth-century fortified
building joined onto the former lighthouse of
the Vieux Port; today this has been adapted into
a bell tower with a pink dome.

The small chapel on the Ilot St-Vincent stands
further out to sea, as does the pier, which offers a
marvellous view of the coastline. Behind the
church, the old Mouré quarter, with its steep
streets running between the sea and the so-called
"Ravin du Douy", faces the Château Royal. The
towering, rose-pink bulk of this building, which

Set in a beautiful location
on the Côte Vermeille, the
streets of Collioure that
attract tourists today drew
painters in the past (*left*).

Collioure's terraced vineyards overlook the creek and town (*right*), where the old lighthouse is now the bell tower of the Church of Notre-Dame des Anges (*far right*).

closes in on its medieval donjon, is anchored to the water's edge. This site has been coveted since antiquity, as it divides the port into two coves. During the thirteenth and fourteenth centuries it was the summer residence of the kings of Majorca,

while under the iron rule of Vauban, it was a key element of Roussillon's seventeenth-century defences and consequently was acquired by France.

Above the beach of the Port-d'Avall, and just below the Gaston-Pams Garden and a path that climbs up to the incredibly beautiful viewpoint at St-Elme Fort, stands the old Dominican church. The region's cooperative cellar is now housed within its thirteenth-century walls.

A difficult terroir

Clinging to the slopes, the vineyards rise above the town and the coast. Underpinned by low stone walls, the narrow soil-covered terraces are moulded onto the schist bedrock and dotted here and there with rare trees. The *vignerons* struggle to produce Roussillon's wines from these work-intensive, scorching terroirs. The wines are surprisingly colourful, vigorous, fleshy, and "natural" – as they were called in the old days to differentiate the red wines from the *vins doux* that are also abundantly produced here.

Wine from the extreme south

On the edge of Spanish Catalonia, Collioure's appellation is superimposed over the Banyuls appellation vineyard. Created in 1971, it took the name of the commune already reputed for its red wines and rosés, leaving the Banyuls name to the *vins doux naturels*, which have had their own AC since 1936. Grenache is the predominant grape here, too, while Mourvèdre or Syrah – varieties that are fresher and less prone to oxidation – are added in variable proportions. Wonderfully suited to the poor, dry terroirs, these grapes produce rich and powerful wines with an elegant structure. Juicy, ripe red and black fruits – namely cherries and blackberries – and notes of spice characterize the aroma of Collioure's red wine, and its full-bodied, velvety texture makes it extremely desirable.

Bergerac

SOUTH WEST

As the Dordogne winds its way across the Bergerac area, twisting and turning towards the Libourne part of Bordeaux, both banks are literally covered in vines. Not a single slope is exempt. Rows of vines grow right up to the first houses on the edges of every village and town. Indeed, viticulture is so important that this southern fringe of the Périgord has been christened the "purple Périgord" – reference to the deep colour of the red wines from the Bergerac area. But it could just as well have been called "golden", as this is the colour of the white wines – often sweet *moelleux* or *liquoreux* – that are produced from Monbazillac to St-Michel-de-Montaigne.

Capital of viticultural Périgord

Bergerac is a truly rich land. Known as the "other" great Aquitaine vineyard, it is the only one that can compete in any realistic way with that of neighbouring Bordeaux. Traversed by such a large river – with an outlet to the Atlantic provided by the Gironde – Bergerac was determined to control the river traffic and the route that crossed from the north bank to the south. Its port played an essential role in the circulation of people and commerce from early in its history; wine and river transportation have always gone well together, and here they were supplemented by tobacco, which was grown in large quantities in the Dordogne from the seventeenth century onwards.

It is obvious from its raised position on a terrace above the Dordogne that the old town was once fortified. However, Louis XIII captured the Protestant stronghold in 1620 and destroyed the ramparts, leaving nothing behind. Yet Bergerac's lengthy prosperity lives on in almost every street, alley, and square, with a dazzling maze of buildings that incorporates every possible shade of warm yellow-ochre. The charm of old half-timbered

houses, mullioned windows, and arcades abundantly fills streets such as the rue St James and the rue des Fontaines, and squares such as the Place de la Myrpe and the Place Pélissière.

A staging post for pilgrims on one of the routes to Santiago de Compostella, Bergerac still has a twelfth-century church dedicated to St James (here called St Jacques), which was restored in the nineteenth century. St Jacques was in fact restored while the neo-Gothic Church of Notre-Dame, with its tall spire, was being built in the upper part of the town.

Visitors interested in wine, however, usually prefer to see the old Récollets Convent built above the disused commercial port, which now houses the Maison des Vins de Bergerac. It has wonderful vaulted cellars, a cloister dating from several periods with an attractive wooden galleried courtyard, and windows that open wide over the river towards Monbazillac and its superb château.

Another attraction is the Maison Peyrarède, an interesting early seventeenth-century town house near the convent, which has been transformed into a fascinating tobacco museum. At the back of the Place de la Myrpe, a delightful half-timbered brick house contains the Musée du Vin, de la Batellerie et de la Tonnellerie (the Wine, River Transport and Cooperage Museum).

Bergerac's interesting waterside façades (*below*) and elegant dwellings (*left*) bear witness to its prosperous history.

The splendid buildings of the quayside (*above*), and the cloister and internal galleried courtyard (*right*) of the Récollets Convent.

The omnipresent vine

The vines begin on the outskirts of Bergerac. Pécharmant is the region's most reputed *cru* – a robust, fleshy red wine famous for keeping well. Its vineyards lie to the east on the gravelly slopes that descend toward the small port at Creysse.

In the north, the surrounding hills form an amphitheatre that dominates the town and valley. In the middle of the many vines dedicated to red wine nestles the small white-wine appellation of Rosette, covering just a few plots. Its traditional *moelleux* wines are light and floral. A larger band of vineyards belonging to the vast Bergerac and Côtes de Bergerac appellations runs alongside the right bank of the Dordogne up to St-Michel-de-Montaigne, which offers lovely views towards the vine-covered slopes of Monbazillac and Saussignac.

The "other" great Aquitaine vineyard

The diversity of Bergerac's wine, spread over both banks of the Dordogne, is certainly impressive, with ninety-three villages and thirteen ACs made up of 12,000 hectares. The grape varieties are the same as those of Bordeaux: Merlot, Cabernet Sauvignon, Malbec, and Cabernet Franc for reds and rosés; Sémillon, Sauvignon, and Muscadelle for the white wines. But the different blends, terroirs, and the orientation of the plots give rise to a range of wines with contrasting personalities. The vineyards produce dry whites as well as sweet white wines that are *moelleux* or *liquoreux*, not only in Bergerac and Côtes de Bergerac, but also in Montravel, Haut-Montravel, Côtes de Montravel Rosette, Saussignac, and Monbazillac. Red wines are also produced in Bergerac and Côtes de Bergerac, as well as Pécharmant and Montravel. All show very generous flavours and honour the varied terroirs that make Bergerac's often forgotten differences count when compared to the wines of neighbouring Bordeaux.

Cahors

SOUTH WEST

Cahors preserves traces of its medieval times, such as the Tour Jean XXII (*right*) and the Pont Valentré that spans the Lot (*far right*).

In a succession of meanders and loops etched with villages and vines, the Lot River makes an amazing journey from east to west across the Quercy and through the *causse*: a wild, arid limestone plateau. Curled up in one of the most charming sites of the valley, the capital, Cahors, sits on an elongated peninsula well-protected by a circle of limestone cliffs known locally as the Cévennes. Powerful throughout the Middle Ages, the city was for some time the important financial seat of Lombardy bankers and the home town of Jacques Duèze, who became the influential Avignon Pope Jean XXII.

Cahors is the main vineyard of this high country and a bountiful producer of strong and flavourful wines which were beloved by a local poet of the early sixteenth-century, Clément Marot. The wine-producing parishes of the valley, stretching from Lamagdelaine to Château de Bonaguil, include Mercuès, Pradines, Trespoux-Rassiels, Douelle, Parnac, St-Vincent-Rive d'Olt, Luzech, Albas, Belaye, Prayssac, Pescadoires, Puy-l'Evêque, Vire-sur-Lot, and Soturac.

Cahors' re-emergence

Despite a great reputation, especially for their so-called "black" wines, the Cahors vineyards nearly disappeared with the attack of phylloxera. Today they are planted mainly on the terraces of ancient alluvial soils in the valley and on the limestone *causse* known as the "white Quercy", on the south of the Lot – to the detriment of the *causse* on the northern bank of the river. Since the 1950s and 1960s, Cahors has progressively recovered its main grape variety, the Auxerrois or Côt Noir, a variety similar to Malbec, which produces rich, well-rounded wines with intense flavours. Merlot and/or Tannat may be blended with it to modulate the style. The wines vary in flexibility; some even keep well, and are an ideal match for the local cuisine which is flavoured with truffles.

At the heart of the Lot Valley

Anchored on the bank of the Lot in the higher part of the vineyards that bear its name, Cahors developed on the eastern side of the river bend during the Middle Ages. The famous Pont Valentré is the symbol of the city and spans the river. With three square towers to protect it, this solid, massive bridge is a fourteenth-century masterpiece of defensive architecture.

The old town retains numerous reminders of its former prosperity: the towering Cathedral of St Etienne, which was built mainly in the twelfth century and is rather bizarrely endowed with two large domes; the Tour de Jean XXII, a last vestige of the Palais Duèze; the Barbacane, a guardroom with its imposing Tour des Pendus (Tower of the Hanged Men), reminiscent of the days when Cahors was a fortified town; the Renaissance house called "Henri IV"; and the houses of the old Baderns or Daurade quarters, built of bricks and timber.

Additionally, many fortified villages and châteaux are scattered throughout the vineyards. They are symbols of the turbulent history of these parts and act as guardians of the vines that cover the terraced slopes of the valley and the higher lands of the *causse*. For centuries, the wines they produce have been firm-bodied with a good colour. Although they were much appreciated, commercial dealings were hampered over the years by Bordeaux's dominance in the wine trade at the mouth of the Lot, which opens into the Garonne. Recently, however, rivalries have become outmoded with the renewed success of Cahors' wines.

Gaillac

SOUTH WEST

At the heart of the Tarn's vineyards (*above*), Gaillac holds a key position on the right bank. Its abbey church borders the river (*right*).

Following the sinuous course of the river Tarn, the soft landscape of small hills and slopes emits a quasi-Mediterranean harmony that makes it hard to imagine anything other than vines ever growing here. The discovery near Gaillac of an amphorae workshop, which was active in Montans from the beginning of the first century AD, strengthens this impression.

All along the river below Albi, villages and towns display stone churches, houses, farms, and pigeon houses built in an infinite variety of shades between rose and ochre. The setting is completed by a geometric pattern of vines alternating with fields of cereal crops.

A diversity of grapes

Throughout its differing terroirs, the Gaillac appellation – covering an area of 1,600 hectares (much less than in previous centuries) – has managed to retain some of its original grape varieties. For white wines, Mauzac usually gives the best sparkling wine produced by the "rural" or "Gaillac" method, as well as the best *moelleux* wines, while the Len-de-l'El and the rare Ondenc that grow alongside Bordeaux varieties Sauvignon, Sémillon, and Muscadelle, keep traditional varieties alive. For the red wines, Duras and Braucol (or Fer) impart a rounded character to wines that may be blended with Syrah, or even Gamay, or other Bordeaux grapes. These local varieties make Gaillac an irreplaceable wine region. Once again, after uncertain times, it has become incredibly precious in the eyes of wine-lovers.

Bridgehead of the high country

The port and town of Gaillac occupy a key position on the right bank of a bend in the Tarn, in the heart of these historical vineyards. Its trading outlet, via the river Garonne and the Atlantic, was hindered for a long time by the privileged position held by Bordeaux, which imposed regular penalties on all upland wines. In spite of this, the conditions were favourable enough to justify the foundation of a successful Benedictine abbey, whose legacy is the mainly Gothic church (with Romanesque origins) of St Michel that watches over the complicated network of streets. Today the abbey buildings house the Maison de la Vigne et du Vin.

Above here, in the old quarter, the Church of St Pierre – built at the same time as the abbey church and also mainly Gothic in style – sits next to the thirteenth- and fifteenth-century Hôtel de Brens. Also of note is the beautifully crafted Château de Foucaud, which elegantly surveys the Tarn from its terraces and park, that were created by the famous garden designer, Le Nôtre.

Multifaceted terroirs

Along the Tarn around Gaillac, the vineyards display many facets in their landscape, terroirs, grape varieties, and wines. The gravelly terraces of the left bank are good for growing red grapes, especially around the village of Cadalen or the Técou *bastide* (fortified medieval new town). The right bank is the more important and supports most of the Tarn's villages, including Gaillac. Downriver is Lisle-sur-Tarn, a *bastide* with old brick-built and half-timbered houses, where the small streets are sometimes bridged by houses and can be arcaded. Rabastens is a small market town with sturdy walls centred around the Church of Notre-Dame-du-Bourg, which boasts a towering, fortified steeple that is a remarkable example of southern Gothic architecture.

Leaving the right bank behind, vines clamber up the slopes of the Premières Côtes, famed for

From a turret overlooking the Tarn (*right*) to a pigeon loft amid the vines (*far right*), the Gaillac area is full of charming treasures.

both its dry and sweet white wines. They then continue over the hills that run the length of the Vère river, which flows along the edges of the Forêt de la Grésigne as far as the extraordinary Puycelsi *bastide*.

The magnificent oak forest, protected in former days by a boundary wall, was requisitioned in the seventeenth century by the French finance minister, Colbert, and reserved for the French Royal Navy.

The rustic beauty of the Premières Côtes and its charming villages make it one of the greatest attractions of the Gaillac area. Some popular stop-offs are Cahuzac-sur-Vère, Broze, Cestayrols, and, to the north on the banks of the Vère, the marvellous fortified Romanesque church at Romanou.

Further north again, the village of Cordes, perched on the Puech de Mordagne peak in an extraordinary site above Cérou, is considered to be the Mont-St-Michel of the Midi. This unaltered thirteenth-century medieval jewel sits on the borders of the Albigeois, Quercy, and Rouergues regions. Its narrow streets are packed with a superb collection of houses and Gothic *hôtels*, contained within successive, concentric ramparts. It is a remarkable treasure in the land of Albigeois *bastides*.

Irouléguy

SOUTH WEST

Irouléguy is full of charm, from the "noble" houses among the vines below the mountain (*above*), to the Basque houses at the foot of the hill slopes (*right*).

century, it then became French Lower Navarre. From that time onwards, the vines nurtured on the slopes of Irouléguy and Anhaux were cut off from their cultivators, the monks of Roncevaux, who from the eleventh century had worked to produce provisions for the crowds of pilgrims on their way to Santiago de Compostella.

Basque above all

In addition to Irouléguy, Anhaux, and Baïgorry, the vineyards now cover Ascarat, Ispoure, Jaxu, St-Martin-d'Arrossa, Ossès, and Bidarray. However, most of the vines are still concentrated on the steep slopes of Jara, the mountain overlooking Irouléguy.

A small Romanesque chapel set apart from the village recalls the old priory, built here by the monks of Roncevaux. Like the façades of the charming Basque houses, the chapel is completely white.

To the west, at the entrance to the Aldudes Valley, the nearby town of Baïgorry has many wonderful aristocratic medieval houses with carved lintels that sit under the watchful eye of the Château d'Atchauz.

A few miles to the east lies St-Jean-Pied-de-Port, a small town full of character and famous in the history of Navarre, with ramparts and a citadel. Lower down, Ossès is filled with outstanding examples of historical rural houses.

Terraces and slopes facing due south have been reclaimed by once forgotten vines, following the decades of decline brought on by crop blight and the general rural exodus. Neat plots now neighbour the pastures that are devoted to a local breed of sheep, the red- or black-headed *manechs*. These sheep supply milk for the *ardi gasna*, an exceptionally delicious local cheese, only rivalled by the celebrated Aldudes *charcuterie* made from black-footed Basque pigs. These two local gastronomic specialties, as well as others, are perfectly complemented by the wine from Irouléguy.

I n the middle of the Basque Country, the village of Roncesvalles, better-known by its French name of Roncevaux, lies hidden behind the Col d'Ibaneta. At the bottom of the mountain, several fast-flowing rivers have created an unusual and picturesque landscape. The Nive des Aldudes crosses St-Etienne-de-Baïgorry, while the Nive de Béhérobie, Nive d'Arnéguy, and Nive de Laurhibar, all join together just below St-Jean-Pied-de-Port to form the Grande Nive, which flows into the Adour at Bayonne before reaching the Atlantic.

The Baïgorry Valley and the lands of Cize and Ossès formed part of the *ultrapuertos* (across the mountains), a region that belonged to Navarre but was far from its capital, Pamplona. Annexed by Henri IV at the beginning of the seventeenth

A rediscovered vineyard

Labelled AC since 1970, the Irouléguy appellation is the last proof – together with the *txakoli* (pronounced *chacolí*) wine produced on the Spanish side – of the extensive Basque vineyards of former times. It was once a veritable museum of the old grape varieties, but today the varieties planted on its 200 hectares are limited to Cabernet Franc, Cabernet Sauvignon, and Tannat for red and rosé wines, and to a lesser extent, Courbu and Petit and Gros Manseng for the whites. A new generation of *vignerons* has given it a new identity, producing compelling wines that are full-bodied, focused, firm, and intensely fruity.

Madiran

SOUTH WEST

Rows of vines clamber over the hills of Vic Bilh (*above*), interspersed with wonderful Gascony farmhouses (*right*), making Madiran's vineyard one of the most attractive in southwest France.

The "Old Country", or *Vic Bilh* in Gascon, is part of the right angle formed by the river Adour at the intersection of the Pyrénées-Atlantiques, the Hautes-Pyrénées, and the Gers. The waters of the river have formed valleys which face west and east, as well as marvellous little slopes facing south in gorges that intersect the mountainside.

In this region, vines have been cultivated through the ages, as can be seen from the eleventh-century sculpture of a *vigneron* in the stone capital of the Madiran priory. But the work undertaken by monks throughout the Middle Ages had all but disappeared by the beginning of the twentieth century.

Today, the vineyard is tended by a handful of tenacious producers who have renewed the postwar success of the earthy red wine, Madiran, as well as the sophisticated and exclusive white, the Pacherenc du Vic Bilh.

Between Madiran and Pacherenc du Vic Bilh

An important staging post on one of the roads leading to the pilgrimage route of Santiago de Compostella, Madiran became a hub of vineyard activity long before giving its name to red wine. The village, with its Benedictine priory, retains the medieval flavour of prosperous times. The ruins of the monastery lie next to the abbey church, a severe eleventh-century building constructed over a superb barrel-vaulted crypt.

On account of the orientation of the diverse terroirs – slopes facing east favour red grapes, while those facing west are more suited to white varieties – the Vic Bilh vineyards are divided into numerous centres around Madiran.

The countryside of the region is carved by small rivers that run parallel to the Adour before rejoining it upstream of d'Aire-sur-Adour. The Bergons bathes the feet of Madiran, while the Saget runs close to Maumusson-Laguian and, together with the Larcis, outlines the Viella, the Aydie, the Arrosès, and the Crouseilles areas. Meanwhile the Lées, more to the west, borders on Portet and Diusse.

Villages and hamlets intersect the valleys within a radius that is rarely more than ten kilometres (six miles). Diusse boasts a beautiful Romanesque church built of sandstone, while Crouseilles is home to an imposing medieval castle. A little further on, the largest and most important cooperatives of the area, both historically and in terms of quantity, are to be found. Finally, at Soublecause, there is a stunning panoramic view of Adour Valley.

One area, two appellations

The same appellation zone licenses the production of Madiran AC for red wine and Pacherenc du Vic Bilh AC for white. Madiran is by far the larger of the two and covers 1,200 hectares. It gains its originality and character from the Tannat, a local grape variety with a strong body and a lot of tannin that is often combined in variable proportions with either of the two Cabernet varieties, Sauvignon or Franc. The Pacherenc du Vic Bilh, whose plots total around 200 hectares and are mixed with those of the Madiran AC, can be dry or *moelleux*, even *liquoreux*, depending on the year and the respective percentages of Arrufiac, Petit Manseng (the most likely to produce rich, unctuous wines), Gros Manseng, and Courbu.

Blaye

BORDEAUX

Blaye's powerful citadel was protected by moats and ditches and spanned by rare crossing points over the Gironde estuary.

If it were true that great rivers historically made great vineyards, then Blaye would stand in an unrivalled position. Situated on the right bank of the Gironde, just beyond the meeting point of the Dordogne and Garonne rivers where the estuary widens before opening into the Atlantic, and downstream from Bordeaux and at the mouth of the Ambès, this village was destined to be the key to the province of Aquitaine. Located on the northwestern point of the huge Libourne region opposite the Médoc, viticulture only added to its commercial and military vocations. One of the greatest charms of the countryside around Blaye is that the rural life of the vineyards – the hills and lush green mounds sprinkled with unassuming villages – blends so harmoniously with the river-based traditions of the Gironde. Fishing shacks on stilts dot the river's edge, with square nets sticking out on the ends of long poles, while opposite, islands stretch out lazily in the current.

Bordeaux citadel

Blaye is strategically located, set on a limestone outcrop just above the Gironde at the entrance to the Saugeron Valley, one of the small valleys on the right bank of the river, bordering the hills of

Blaye appellations

At one time Blaye was a source of neutral white grapes used for distillation in nearby Cognac, before it slipped into the production of negligible white wines and anonymous red clarets. But Blaye has now successfully restored its reputation – one of the oldest in Bordeaux. Red wines give the area its importance, with Premières Côtes de Blaye AC made from Merlot, with Cabernet Sauvignon and sometimes Cabernet Franc or Malbec. Premières Côtes de Blaye AC whites are Sauvignon Blanc-based, with a little Sémillon and Muscadelle. Good AC Côtes de Blaye and AC Blaye dry whites are also produced. Made in classical Bordeaux style, Blaye wines embody nuances of their terroir, heightened by a genuine desire for rebirth.

Bourg and Blaye. At first it was a Roman camp, then the site of a medieval castle, whose ruins evoke memories of Jaufré Rudel, Prince of Blaye, a twelfth-century musician and troubadour.

In the seventeenth century, under the orders of Louis XIV, the promontory was developed into a large, powerful citadel and the king's architect, Vauban, created this city within a city. Together with the fort on the l'Ile Pâté and Fort Médoc on the far side of the river, Blaye guarded the estuary.

There are many old dwellings and buildings, such as the house of the commander at arms, (now the Musée du Pays Blayais), the Convent of Minimes, and the powder house. These are all tightly packed within the strong fortification walls, which are surrounded by moats and ditches and pierced by two gates: the Porte Royale and the Porte Dauphine. The walls are punctuated with bastions and towers – the Tour des Rondes and Tour de l'Aiguillette – and preceded by sloping banks, upon one of which sits the small, walled Echaugette Clos.

The lower part of the town curls its narrow streets and old houses around the foot of the citadel. Beyond, the vineyards take possession of a gently sloping countryside where village buildings present their own history: Gallo-Roman villas in Plassac; Romanesque churches at Cars, St-Martin-Lacaussade, and Cartelègue; and fortified houses such as the Château Boisset in Berson.

Just down river from Bordeaux, Blaye boasts an ideal location and has a long tradition as the capital of these vineyards.

Fronsac

BORDEAUX

A tiny town on the edge of the Dordogne at the foot of the slopes, Fronsac occupies one of the most picturesque sites in Bordeaux.

Fronsac is literally a "high point" of the area, conspicuously located on top of a small hill amid the gentle surrounding countryside of the alluvial plain. Sitting on an outcrop where the meandering Isle River joins the Dordogne just after Libourne, it has been the object of military and commercial desires throughout history.

The site was converted from the time when Charlemagne placed a fortress on the hill at Fronsac, long before Libourne or St-Emilion became important. It was the Duke of Fronsac,

Twin appellations

The Fronsac vineyard comprises two ACs. Firstly, the Canon-Fronsac AC covers 308 hectares around Fronsac and St-Michel-de-Fronsac, and secondly the Fronsac AC makes up a total of about 840 hectares extending north and west to St-Aignan, Saillans, Galgon, La Rivière, and St-Germain-la-Rivière. Merlot is king here, with the addition of Cabernet Franc, Cabernet Sauvignon, and a little Malbec. The St-Emilion and the Pomerol vineyards lie further to the west, beyond the Isle. Fronsac and Canon-Fronsac are today regaining their own personalities. Their wines are fruity, heavy, and well-rounded, with a firm – sometimes "rustic" – structure, which makes these good for laying down. The characteristic flavour of the terroir adds to the quiet charm of the region's wine.

Richelieu's great nephew, and Richelieu himslef, who launched Fronsac's wine in the eighteenth century. He saw the big Libournais landowners producing wine of quality in the surrounding area, soon extending over all of Libourne.

A charming landscape

Low plots and embankments on the river precede a landscape of small hills, valleys, and natural terraces. This undulating countryside, scattered with groups of trees and copses, is undeniably one of the prettiest in Bordeaux.

Today, the hill is crowned with a house built in the style of the Second Empire, set amid its

grounds. The village at the foot of the hill is built around a small Romanesque church, behind the small port, which has been obsolete for some time.

While the main activities take place in the surrounding châteaux and estates, the small town of Fronsac itself remains a charming, tranquil place. The picturesque hills, which face the Dordogne, are famed for their sluggish slopes, known as *du Fronsadais* ("from the Fronsac area"), formed of sandy clay soils in varying proportions. These, along with the eroded limestone plateau that extends to its summit, provide the best Fronsac terroirs.

The vineyards begin northwest of Fronsac and spread east toward the St-Michel-de-Fronsac commune, taking in the famous mound of Tertre de Canon, to whose name several châteaux have laid claim. Due to its exceptional features, this zone has its own appellation, Canon-Fronsac, and is differentiated from the Fronsac AC. The vineyards continue toward the village of La Rivière, whose magnificent château – which has changed hands frequently since the seventeenth century – is majestically located in a vast, natural amphitheatre with a wooded crown, and lies between the vines of the plateau and those of the small round hills.

Small valleys and rounded hills create a countryside full of charm, as well as some of the best wines of Libourne.

Margaux

BORDEAUX

A church amid the vines symbolizes the exclusive vocation of a village famous for its wine-growing châteaux, such as the prestigious Château Margaux (*right*).

I f "Médoc is the Versailles of wine", as was declared by the acclaimed wine writer Hugh Johnson, then likewise, Margaux is the Versailles of the Médoc. This is the heart of pure wine classicism, with its measured composition, its balance, and the restrained elegance that is often considered to define the French idea of "good taste".

Château Margaux

Margaux is not the only village under the Margaux AC, which also includes Cantenac as well as Arsac, Labarde, and Soussans. It is, however, indisputably the most famous estate. Designated a *premier cru classé*, it stands at the head of around twenty other estates labelled as second, third, fourth, or fifth *crus* in the AC. Like them, it is mainly planted with Cabernet Sauvignon grapes, together with some Merlot, and a little Cabernet Franc and Petit Verdot, on average-sized, abundant gravel stones. The early nineteenth-century château, at the top of a long entrance lined

with plane trees, is the work of Emile Combes, who studied under the French architect Victor Louis. Inspired by the work of the sixteenth-century Italian architect Andrea Palladio, it is in the austere, formal neoclassical style. Stairs lead up to a formal front entrance with four ionic columns. The same architect designed the vast wine store divided by eighteen columns, an orangery, a pavilion for the estate manager, the "craftsmen's courtyard" with workshops (including the estates own barrel-maker), and the "village street", bordered by around thirty dwellings for housing the staff.

It was in the second half of the seventeenth century, continuing into the eighteenth century, that Médoc in general and Margaux in particular rose to the top of the wine hierarchy. Château Margaux was built at the height of the neoclassical revival of the nineteenth century, right in the centre of its prestigious estate and the commune of Margaux's appellation.

Aristocratic vineyard

Before the Médoc area was converted into vineyards, the land, while owned by the aristocracy, was largely shared between market gardeners and farmers of cereal crops. Viticulture, however, wound up firmly in the hands of the wealthy owners of huge estates and the church. Thus, from the end of the sixteenth century, the seigniory of La Mothe de Margaux (which was to become Château Margaux) and the nearby Priory of Cantenac (the future Château Prieuré-Lichine) both began developing vineyards, foreshadowing the somewhat frenzied planting of vines in the area which occurred in the eighteenth century.

The landscape opens up as you approach the village from the direction of Bordeaux. The gravelly plateau is so completely covered in vines that its soft mounds are only discernible from the undulating lines of the neatly spaced plants.

Margaux exemplifies wine production in the Médoc. The village is rural and rather modest, but it is not the real centre of Margaux. Instead, its districts are divided and arranged around the most important château, Château Margaux, as well as the châteaux of Malescot-St-Exupéry, Durfort-Vivens, Rausan-Ségla, Rauzan-Gassies, Château Palmer in the hamlet of Issan, Château Lascombes, and Château Labégorce. Even the eighteenth-century church was placed symbolically in the middle of the vineyards – closer to Château Margaux than to the village.

St-Emilion

BORDEAUX

Right in the heart of the old town, the Eglise Monolith (Monolithic Church) occupies a special place in the life of St-Emilion.

One of the most exalted places in the Bordeaux region, or more precisely, the Libourne – a large area on the right bank of the Garonne – St-Emilion occupies a privileged position overlooking the Dordogne. The town is situated on a limestone hilltop opposite the more imposing Graves and Médoc estates.

Anchored to the traditions of the land, St-Emilion watches over the large vineyards that surround it on all sides. There is no better viewpoint than that from the top of the Tour du Roy, which is all that remains of a thirteenth-century castle. This tower is the traditional location for the ceremonial harvest proclamation, made by the Jurade de St-Emilion. This association, created in 1199, was once all-powerful, but is today mainly ceremonial. The entire village is visible from the tower, and beyond that, the surrounding countryside dotted is with châteaux carrying famous names.

Heritage town

The wealth of historic and cultural treasures in this medieval jewel is such that St-Emilion has been awarded World Heritage Site status by UNESCO. To begin with, there is the extraordinary Eglise Monolith (Monolithic Church, the most important of its kind in France and the most impressive. Dating from the eleventh and twelfth centuries, it is carved out of the limestone rock characteristic of the area. This underlying rock is rich in galleries that originally supplied the town with building materials before they became used as ideal cellars for maturing and

storing wine. The church has three vast underground naves, a Romanesque tympanum, and a tall steeple rising above it. Built around the same time, the collegiate church was probably built from stone extracted from the monolith.

Along the steep, winding streets, many buildings bear witness to the prosperity of the town, which was amply protected by strong fortifications with many gates. Outside the walls, the vestigial remains such as the *grandes murailles* ("great walls") are evidence of the dominant role played by various religious orders. This is the last remaining stretch of wall belonging to the old Jacobin Monastery, the local name for the Dominicans.

Between the plateau and the hills, St-Emilion overlooks a rural landscape devoted exclusively to grape-growing.

St-Emilion retains the appearance of a well-to-do Aquitaine market town, with creamy limestone buildings lining its steep streets.

Diverse terroirs, diverse wines

The complexity of the various terroirs of the area, which spreads over 5,400 hectares, creates great diversity in the many wines they produce. The presence of limestone is the greatest unifying characteristic of the appellation. Another is the use of Merlot, the main grape variety, blended with Cabernet Franc (known here as Bouchet) and often finished with Cabernet Sauvignon or perhaps Malbec (more unusual today). The proportion of the varieties used by an estate varies according to the soil and the situation of the vineyard. To simplify things, these conditions can be grouped into three principle types:
• a limestone plateau that stretches west over an area of ancient sandy shores;
• hills and foothills, two areas that produce the best St-Emilion *crus;*
• sandy alluvial soil of the plain that produces lighter wines than those of the plateau or the hills.

A hierarchy of *cru* classifications crowns the wines produced by the appellation and corresponds to the large range of St-Emilion wines born of these different soils. From the bottom, they are: the *grands crus;* the *grands crus classés;* the *premiers grands crus classés B* (Angélus, Beauséjour-Bécot, Beauséjour, Belair, Canon, Figeac, La Gaffelière, Magdelaine, Pavie, Trottevieille, Clos Fourtet); and, right at the very top, the two single *premiers grands crus classés,* Ausone and Cheval Blanc. The wines from St-Emilion are generous, quite full-bodied, and distinguished by a deep bouquet. The best *crus* also show a marriage of delicacy and strength. They are sometimes quite robust but well-rounded and velvety thanks to the Merlot, and generally more compelling that those from the left banks of the Garonne and Gironde.

Prestigious châteaux

St-Emilion's wealth comes, of course, from its wine. Vineyards surround the town, with the first rows beginning immediately at the threshold of the town gates. To the south, châteaux have been built up over the years along the hills and the edges of the plateau above the Dordogne plain, from Château Pavie, Château Ausone, and Château Belair to Château La

Gaffelière, and Château Magdelaine. Towards the west, Château Canon and Clos Fourtet inhabit the plateau, while right up at the northern limits, before the territory of Pomerol begins, are the famous Château Figeac and Château Cheval Blanc. These are the greatest St-Emilion terroirs that produce the appellation's most reputed wines. Although known for some time previously, these wines only came into their full glory during the nineteenth century. Vineyards also cover larger, less prestigious estates and terroirs to the north, the east, and in the south, but whatever their standing, the wines produced here take the names of their respective villages to the wider world. They are all enhanced by St-Emilion's identity and consequently possess a place at the heart of myriad wines produced in Bordeaux.

In the depths of the calcareous underground, galleries with massive pillar supports have become ideal wine cellars for St-Emilion wine.

St-Macaire

BORDEAUX

Today, the former port of St-Macaire, with its old houses clustered along the bank of the Garonne, is the charming "capital" of a small, discrete wine appellation.

St-Macaire occupies a remarkably strategic position. The small, fortified town is fixed to a limestone outcrop opposite Langlon, at the southern gateway to Bordeaux's wine-growing region. It is situated between Premières Côtes de Bordeaux and Entre-deux-Mers on the one hand and Graves on the other.

Long before the river changed course, leaving the quayside several hundred metres inland, it was a key port on the Garonne. During Bordeaux's "privileged" era, wines from the upper part of the country – particularly those from Cahors and Gaillac transported along the Lot and the Tarn – had to wait for permission to access the great port on the Gironde, where they were marketed. Naturally enough, priority was accorded to wines from St-Macaire produced on the right bank, but also to the Bordeaux from Ste-Croix-du-Mont, Loupiac, and Cadillac, to the wines of the Entre-deux-Mers area, and to those on the opposite bank from Graves and Sauternes.

Southern gateway to Bordeaux

On account of its importance, St-Macaire was well-fortified. Today, these fortifications can still be discerned from the layout of the old town. Old houses and narrow streets are squeezed around the imposing twelfth- and fourteenth-century Church of St-Sauveur, as well as the main remaining building of the Romanesque cloister. They also surround the Benedictine priory that was built on top of the hermitage of St Macaire, the local preacher and patron saint of the commune.

Sweet white specialties

Alongside its simple red clarets and dry white wines, St-Macaire stands out for its production of a small quantity of *moelleux* and *liquoreux* white wines that have been accorded the Côtes de Bordeaux St-Macaire AC. Like other neighbouring sweet wines on both sides of the Garonne, these come mainly from the Sémillon grape and are finished with Sauvignon or Muscadelle, from which they gain floral and honey flavours – quite different to the rather ordinary tastes they had not so very long ago. These smooth and mellow wines deserve to be better-known.

Other than the Porte de Turon and Porte de Rendesse gates, the main entrance into the town was via the Porte de Benauge, a belfry built during the thirteenth and fourteenth centuries and decorated with a clock. At the heart of the old quarter is the Place du Mercadiou (from *marché Dieu* – "God's marketplace"). Houses and Gothic

dwellings with wide stone arcades surround this large space and present the image of a bustling commercial town, typical of Bordeaux.

The gently undulating southeastern vineyard boundary, which stretches between the Garonne and the Dordogne, models the Côtes de Bordeaux landscape. It is completely covered with vines, offset by a few charming parishes. St-Maixant is home to Malagar, the famous dwelling beloved by the novelist François Mauriac, while the Château de Malromé, set apart from the village of St-André-du-Bois, was home to the painter Toulouse-Lautrec before his death. He is buried a few miles away in Verdelais.

Sauternes

BORDEAUX

Château d'Yquem, Sauterne's emblematic château, is one of the great mystical estates in the world of wine.

Situated in the undulating landscape between the Ciron and Garonne rivers, Sauternes has become synonymous with the phrase "the greatest sweet wine in the world". On autumn nights before the harvest, the two rivers wrap the vineyards in a humid mist that is gradually dispersed during the day by the sun. This humidity creates the particular conditions that are needed to form the famous "noble rot" on the grapes – a feature of all truly great sweet white wines.

The essential nature of "noble rot"

The villages that make up the Sauternes AC (wines from Barsac have the right of opting for a special label, AC Barsac) all share a ponderous clay-based calcareous soil and grow a mixture of grape varieties largely dominated by Sémillon and balanced with Sauvignon and Muscadelle in varying proportions. In the particular mesoclimate of the region, and in favourable years these grapes – especially Sémillon – are sensitive to the *Botrytis cinerea* fungus which grows on healthy grapes and generates a type of rot known as "noble". At the end of several selective harvests conducted by hand, this produces grapes with a very high sugar and glycerol content. The wine that is made from these grapes, in vastly reduced quantities, is sweet, rich, and thick – unctuous and of great aromatic complexity.

The capital of sweet wine

The art of making sweet wine was only truly mastered on the banks of the Gironde from the seventeenth century onwards – in the same era as when the neighbouring Graves wines became widely celebrated and when the townspeople of Bordeaux began to settle in Sauternes' "noble establishments". Today, Sauternes remains a modest village centred around its church, which has an original Romanesque chancel with seventeenth- and ninteenth-century additions. The real riches, however, can be found

at the châteaux and occasional castles that are dotted around the heart of this gently rolling viticultural landscape. Their names are on the lips of wine-lovers the world over, but perhaps the best-known is Château d'Yquem: a unique estate, classed as a *premier cru supérieur*. It is a robust sixteenth-century château (with fifteenth-century towers) that has been the property of the Lur-Saluces family since the eighteenth century. From the dawn of the history of great sweet wines, Château d'Yquem has been the established model of a perfect Sauterne wine. Château Guiraud (*premier cru classé*) has an eighteenth-century edifice; Château Filhot (*deuxième cru classé*) boasts aristocratic eighteenth- and ninteenth-century architecture; while the fifteenth-century Château Lamothe (*deuxième cru classé*) is well-situated on top of a hill; as is Château d'Arche (*deuxième cru classé*). These are just a few of the leading names, but there are numerous other châteaux spread over the neighbouring communes of Bommes, Fargues, Preignac, and Barsac which also belong to the Sauternes appellation.

In the middle of a vineyard scattered with prestigious châteaux, Sauternes maintains the appearance of a modest rural village.

Ancenis

LOIRE VALLEY

With its quaysides along the Loire (*above*), Ancenis once held a powerful position. The vineyards that slope towards the river (*right*) continue to bridge the transition between Anjou and Nantes.

On the last leg of a long journey, the Loire leaves Anjou for Brittany, flowing across the country around Nantes before it reaches the ocean. Natural features of the environment determined where the riverside towns and villages would develop, with Ingrandes and Ancenis on the right bank of the river, St-Florent-le-Vieil and Champtoceaux on the left.

The uninterrupted string of islands that stretch into the river – often desolate but for poplars – adds to the valley's charm. Names such as Île Batailleuse, Île Mocquart, Île Kerguelin, Île aux Moines, and Île Coton evoke the land brought to life by the Renaissance poet Joachim du Bellay, born in Liré (his "dear little Liré") at the Château de la Turmelière on the left bank opposite Ancenis.

Watching over the Loire

Distinguished by its position on a hilltop, Ancenis was ideally suited to become the site of castle charged with keeping watch over the river and Brittany's eastern extremities. From the early Middle Ages it was a place of repute.

Renaissance buildings can still be seen, such as the two fifteenth-century entrance towers with their fine example of a covered drawbridge, as well as a section of the heavily fortified walls.

The quayside on the banks of the Loire was frequented by barges transporting barrels of wine for many years and, together with the bridge, symbolizes the east-to-west and south-to-north crossings that brought wealth to the village.

In the quarter of the rue des Tonneliers, picturesque medieval houses, cellars, and mansions endowed with marvellous gates that open onto inner courtyards – the properties of the négociants in the eighteenth century – bear witness to the town's prosperity. And looking over all of this is the unusual fifteenth- and sixteenth-century gated bell tower of the Church of St Pierre-et-Paul.

The Ancenis vineyard is where the "Atlanticized" Loire becomes Breton. Scarcely has the Anjou Coteaux de la Loire appellation ended than the reign of the Melon variety that produces the Muscadet Coteaux de la Loire appellation begins.

Wines of the Coteaux d'Ancenis, an appellation that began as a VDQS, sustain the popularity of the Anjou grape varieties. These vines love the gentle slopes of the river banks. On the western boundary of Ancenis, they surround the village of St-Géréon, where a sheer rock face dominates the Pierre-Meslière slopes. They continue, skirting Oudon and its polygonal sixteenth-century tower, and dawdle on the southern bank around Liré before returning to the northern bank at Cellier. Here they contrast with the fabulous, strange nineteenth-century gardens at Folies-Siffait, which strike an extravagant note in an otherwise serene rural setting.

Straddling the traditions of Anjou and Nantes

The Loire region is best-known for producing dry white wine made from Muscadet grapes, yet in the eastern tip of the western reaches, the appellation Muscadet Coteaux de la Loire yields fuller-bodied wines that are more upfront and earthy than those of the Muscadet de Sèvre-et-Maine appellation. However, to the east, a more traditional selection of the grape varieties is used to make a variety of wines under the Coteaux d'Ancenis appellation: Gamay, Cabernet Franc, and Sauvignon for reds and rosés; Pinot Gris, Malvoisie (Malvasia), and Chenin Blanc for the whites.

Azay-le-Rideau

LOIRE VALLEY

A diamond "set in the Indres" is how the nineteenth-century novelist Balzac described the Château d'Azay-le-Rideau, which is built where it can be gracefully and serenely mirrored by the water. The town on the right bank of the river lives for the château and its success as a tourist destination.

The other local treasure is the vineyards. They surround the town and stretch out towards the Loire along roads that lead to Vallères and Lignières-de-Touraine. Further afield, other famous Loire Valley châteaux may be found at Villandry and Langeais. On the left bank, the vines follow the river down as far as Cheillé and Rivarennes in the direction of d'Ussé and its château, and upriver as far as Saché.

The graceful Loire region

The Château d'Azay-le-Rideau reflects the aristocratic calm of this gentle, luminous country, which was long-cherished by kings and princes, especially in the early sixteenth century. This was the era when Gilles Berthelot, treasurer to François I, replaced the ruins of an old castle,

Azay-le-Rideau, a charming village on the edge of the river Indre, symbolizes the characteristic spirit and elegance of the Loire Valley.

A small original appellation

Touraine wine is a recognized specialty of the Azay-le-Rideau region, but only a small area – around sixty hectares – bears the specific Touraine-Azay-le-Rideau appellation. Produced from chalky soils marled with clay or flint, the white wines, like those of Vouvray and Montlouis, are made solely from the Chenin grape variety. The rosés use mainly Grolleau (or Gros Lot), a grape variety from Cinq-Mars-la-Pile, a village on the northern bank of the Loire. Red wines are made with Gamay, Cabernet Franc, and Côt, and come under the large Touraine appellation. The lively white wines have nuances of acacia and wild roses with subtle mineral overtones. They mature well, acquiring honey and quince flavours. The pale, fresh rosés combine fruity notes of cherries, raspberries, and pears, and floral notes of roses and lilacs with a hint of pepper.

located at the end of an island in the river Indres with a new stately home. The building was Italianate in style and is an early Renaissance masterpiece. Built in an 'L' shape, the southern façade of the château is reflected in the calm water, while its white stonework and blue slate roof stand out against the Touraine skies. Elegant, with harmonious proportions, the château has not lost its appeal despite the passing of time.

The charm of the château is emphasized by that of the land that surrounds it. Azay-le-Rideau is a peaceful place, the countryside gently defined by the great green ribbon of the valley, the undulating vines, the distant woods, and the watermills.

This serene way of life doubtlessly inspired the first *vignerons* to plant their vines on the tranquil banks of the Indre, a cradle of early Touraine viticulture. It is easy to imagine the early wine-growers living and working on troglodyte (cave-like) farms such as the amazing ones at Goupillières, just three kilometres (1.86 miles) from Azay. Since then, these privileged vineyard plots have always been known for the delicate flavour of their wine, especially of their whites and rosés.

The Château d'Azay-le-Rideau, a Renaissance masterpiece, is one of the most famous jewels in this "valley of the kings".

Cheverny

LOIRE VALLEY

The formal architecture of Château de Cheverny (*above*) contrasts with the rural houses dotted among Touraine's vineyards (*right*).

Between the rivers Loire and Cher, south of Blois and Chambord, the area known as the Touraine (the area around Tours) merges with that of the Sologne to form a combination of forests, wooded hunting grounds, heathland, market gardens, orchards, and vines. In the heart of this countryside stands Cheverny, a château that boasts a living tradition of hunting with hounds, and a vineyard with a wonderful range of Touraine wines. The château captures the essence of this charming and often melancholic area that the French historian, Michelet, called a "soft and sensual land".

An emblematic château

The Château de Cheverny stands on the outskirts of the village. Built in a strictly classical style, it is a fine example of early seventeenth-century architecture. Perfectly symmetrical, the narrow central section is framed by two lower wings and finished by two large pavilions, each topped with a dome and a pierced bell tower. The long structure harmoniously combines elegant, white stone – brought from Bourré in the nearby Cher Valley – with a grey-blue slated roof. On the main façade, continuous blocks of plain relief carving accentuate the structure's horizontal calm and contrast with the rhythm of the roofs and chimneys.

The interior is warm, attractive, and more ornate. Its sumptuous furnishings and rich decorations are seductive, particularly the dining room, the grand drawing room, the king's bedchamber, and the guardroom. Visitors are often overawed by the Trophy Room, where around two thousand sets of antlers are displayed, and by the deafening noise of the pack of hounds in the kennels.

Confronted with such opulence, it is almost easy to forget Cheverny village and the larger adjoining market town of Cour-Cheverny. Both are humble in comparison with the château, each centred around a Romanesque church, and boast rustic rather than aristocratic charms. They combine two tightly interwoven appellations in a shared vineyard. In one direction the vines follow the river Beuvon, skirting Cellettes and passing the elegant Renaissance Château de Beauregard before rejoining the Loire toward Candé-sur-Beuvron. In the other direction, they extend towards the powerful medieval fortress of Fougères-sur-Bièvre, passing the magnificent Troussay Manor. This area offers a unique trail for the visitor as a châteaux route and wine route in one.

One vineyard, two appellations

The vineyards that stretch along level with Blois, south of the Loire, are planted with typical Touraine grape varieties. The Cheverny AC was created in 1993. Throughout some twenty-four communes, it comprises wine made from a selected blend of grapes: Sauvignon with a touch of Chardonnay for the whites; and full-bodied Gamay and Pinot Noir supported by Cabernet Franc and Côt for the reds (and for the rosés, which are similar to Pineau d'Aunis). More unusually – and unique in its type – the Cour-Cheverny AC is limited to eleven communes within the same geographic zone which are planted only with the rare Romorantin grape. This white variety, perhaps of old Burgundian origins, has an assertive character and evolves interesting acacia, honey, and waxy nuances with age.

Chinon

LOIRE VALLEY

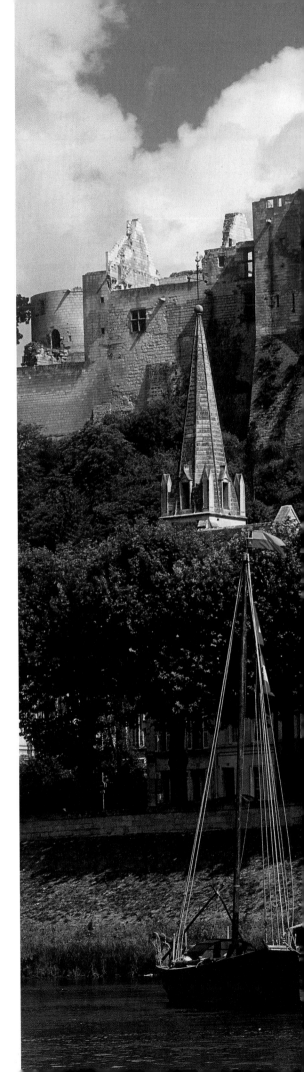

"Small town, great renown," proclaimed the sixteenth-century French writer Rabelais, who was born in the neighbouring smallholding Devinière, several kilometres southwest of Chinon. Established in an exceptional location on the right bank of the Vienne – just upstream from where it meets the Loire – on the Touraine and Anjou border, Chinon boasts a long history and is rich in architecture of the past.

Medieval city

The rhythm of life in Chinon has been punctuated by encounters with history and royalty. Dominating the town are the ruins of a huge mass of fortified buildings that retain impressive elements of all the prestigious eras, with ramparts and donjons from the twelfth, thirteenth, and fourteenth centuries.

The medieval town that developed below the castle between the hillside and the river, still has a strong historical feel to it. The stone used for building was quarried from numerous underground galleries, many of which have become cellars, such as the famous Caves Painctes, which Rabelais loved so much.

The impressive ruins of the castle at Chinon dominate the banks of the Vienne and evoke the town's historical importance.

The kingdom of Cabernet Franc

Chinon's vineyards cover about 2,000 hectares and surround the town on all sides. The varied terroirs include terraces with gravelly and sandy soils near the watercourses that produce light, fruity, delicious wines which are usually ready to drink by the Easter following the harvest. Meanwhile, grapes grown on the chalky clay and flinty clay slopes and plateaus produce wines that remain aromatic but are somewhat firmer, with supple tannins which need time to soften. Many *vignerons* – like those at Cravant-les-Coteaux – own several types of plots and blend the grapes to form a single harmonious vintage. In Chinon, as throughout the Loire Valley, Cabernet Franc is the main grape variety used for producing red wine. Locally called "Breton", The grape originated in Aquitaine, but arrived through the port of Nantes before being imported into the Loire Valley. Its aromatic qualities range from flowers (irises, poppies and violets) to fruits (raspberries, strawberries, and redcurrants). The most complex wines develop velvety textures and woody, mushroom nuances. There is also a rare white Chinon, made, like all the great white Loire Valley wines, from Chenin Blanc grapes.

Old houses are packed tightly into streets that wind towards the centre of the fortified town around squares such as the Grand Carroi, and churches such as the Church of St Maurice, the collegiate Church of St Mexme and the Church of St Etienne, where the Romanesque style sits beside that of Anjou Gothic. Renaissance and seventeenth-century mansions are symbols of the wealth of Chinon's ancient nobility.

The spirit of Chinon

From early in its history, vines surrounded the lively, commercial town of Chinon and there are wine-growing terroirs on every side. The "good Véron countryside", so dear to Rabelais, forms a gently undulating region around Savigny and Beaumont in an arrow-shaped piece of land between the Loire and the Vienne.

From the outskirts of Chinon, south-facing terraces and sloping vineyards follow one another along the right bank of the Vienne. This is home to the famous walled vineyards of Clos de l'Echo and Clos de l'Olive, and in the villages above, Cravant-les-Coteaux and Panzoult. On the opposite bank, resolutely turning its back on Chinon, the plateau surrounding Ligré also faces south.

The diverse nature of Chinon's appellation terroirs creates a diversity of wine styles, from those that are to be enjoyed immediately to others which have been designed to age for several years. Like the works of Rabelais, they are all firmly anchored in the spirit of the place.

Saumur

LOIRE VALLEY

A wonderful town on the banks of the Loire (*above*), Saumur prides itself on its elegant château (*right*).

Today, the Château de Saumur looks much as it did when it was painted in the *Très Riches Heures du Duc de Berry*, an early fifteenth-century Book of Hours written for the Duke of Berry. The proud, elegant castle sits on a promontory overlooking the Loire and can be seen from afar by approaching visitors. Known as "the pearl of Anjou", Saumur holds a key location at the point where the river meets the Thouet and was therefore a natural spot for navigation in bygone days.

With the magnificence of its counts, dukes, and kings, the excellence of its famous Cadre Noir riding school, and the skill of its great wine-producing companies, the town of Saumur lacks very little in terms of prestige.

Saumur: "the white town"

In contrast to Angers, known as the "the black town" on account of the dark colour of the schist from which its castle is built, Saumur is called "white" after the tufa stone that is visible everywhere in the local architecture. The town has prospered century after century and has gained numerous treasures, not least the castle, a fabulous fourteenth-century square building with four corner towers. It now houses the Musée des Arts Décoratifs (Museum of Decorative Arts) and the Musée du Cheval (Horse Museum), and above all offers a magnificent view over the Loire and Thouet valleys.

In addition, remains of the village's fifteenth- and sixteenth-century ramparts and fortifications have survived. Historical towers include the Tour Grenetière and the Tour du Bourg, while streets rich in old houses include "King René's House" and a house on the Île d'Offard associated with the Queen of Sicily.

Also of interest are Saumur's churches. St Pierre is a mixture of Romanesque and Gothic styles, built below the castle on a square filled with charming fifteenth-century half-timbered houses. Notre-Dame de Nantilly is a powerful, solid twelfth-century sanctuary located behind the castle in what is doubtless the oldest part of the citadel. Finally, the sixteenth- and seventeenth-century Church of Notre-Dame des Ardilliers, with its strong classical architecture, affirms a Catholic presence in this Protestant bastion.

Vines and cellars

Throughout the length of the Saumur region, on the sloping hillside of the Loire's right bank, innumerable and often massive caves have been dug out of the limestone tufa. They were mostly quarried to provide stone for the local construction industry, meaning that the castles, manor houses, and other dwellings of the area were literally born from the hollows which today shelter their wines.

To the northwest, St-Florent was formally the seat of an important twelfth-century abbey, of which only attractive ruins now remain, while St-Hilaire was once called St-Hilaire-des-Grottes. These two villages, merged together and linked to Saumur, offer a fabulous network of underground galleries that are ideal for the

development of effervescent wine, as well as for cultivating button mushrooms. Following the example of Jean Ackerman, the first person to make sparkling Saumur in 1811, the two villages made a name for themselves by welcoming prestigious companies to come and make sparkling Saumur wines in their caves.

The other villages in the Saumur zone are not to be outdone, however. Spread out to the southeast of the town, they share vineyard plots planted with white or red grapes, depending on their soil. All of them nurture secret cellars that are each more extraordinary than the next: Dampierre; Souzay-Champigny; Parnay; Turquant on the edge of the "hills"; Varrains; Chaintré; Chacé, with the Musée du Champigny; Champigny, which gave its name to the Saumur-Champigny label; and St-Cyr-en-Bourg, with its huge cooperative cellar.

The network of underground caves dug out of tufa are ideal for making wine – as well as for growing mushrooms.

Still and sparkling wine

A great many wines carry the Saumur name, but what has made the Saumur vineyards most famous – before Saumur-Champigny became the star – is undeniably its sparkling wines, which comprise the greater part of the production. Using a Chenin base finished off with Chardonnay and possibly Sauvignon, or even red grape varieties, the Saumur Mousseux AC – familiarly known as Saumur Brut – is made using the *méthode champenoise*. There is also a minor production of AC Saumur Pétillant, made with less fizz, and more importantly the Crémant de Loire AC, which has extremely rigorous production rules. In each case, these wines offer a strong yet tender character, with flavours typical of Loire white wines grown on limestone tufa.

Savennières

LOIRE VALLEY

An attractive Angevin village set amid vineyards, Savennières clings to the right bank of the Loire.

This is doubtless one of the most beautiful sites of the Loire Valley. Below Angers, Savennières sits in a curve of the river dotted with islands, where the *nautonniers* (boatmen) of the old days guided their sailing barges across the sand banks. Opposite the superb *corniche Angevin* (cliffs of Angers), created by the left bank and the Île Béhuard, the attractive undulations of the right bank surround Savennières. Its outline is accentuated by hedgerows, woodland copses, and the orderly layout of vines covering south-facing slopes which survey the Loire below. The overall picture is of a landscape that is open yet intimate – a perfect example of the "gentle Angevin" so dear to the Renaissance poet Joachim du Bellay.

Anjou's prestigious AC

The Savennières AC is the aristocrat of Anjou viticulture. These wines are exclusively white, born of the noble Chenin Blanc variety. Almost always dry nowadays, they can nevertheless, according to tradition, be *moelleux*. Lively, mineral, but full and robust, they need to mature for several years in order to reveal their full complexity. The wines attain their most sumptuous expression in the two *crus* situated at the east of the appellation on the slopes over the Loire: the Roche-aux-Moines, where the slopes are shared between several owners, and the famous Coulée de Serrant, a single estate on the neighbouring slope, located in front of the Château de la Roche-aux-Moines.

Highlight of the Angevin Loire

Throughout history, man and vine have prospered in this privileged location. On the hillside amid picturesque old houses with slate roofs, stands Anjou's earliest and most beautiful pre-Romanesque church. Some remnants of fine herringbone brickwork are preserved that predate other twelfth-century sections – such as the choir and the bell tower – as well as fifteenth-century additions.

In the middle of the Loire, the Ile Béhuard offered a base for river crossings to Rochefort-

sur-Loire before the bridge was built. This island has kept its traditional reverence for the Virgin Mary, a practice which, in bygone days, was so important for the mariners who faced the dangers of the river on a daily basis.

Louis XI himself miraculously survived a shipwreck in the Loire and commissioned the Notre-Dame de Béhuard to be built in the fifteenth century. The church is surrounded by a charming collection of small streets, whose houses date from the fifteenth to the seventeenth centuries.

The Savennières countryside attracted various princes through the ages. Evidence of their partiality for the place can be seen in the variety of châteaux and beautiful stately homes here. The grand Renaissance Château de Serrant near St-Georges-sur-Loire is surrounded by a water-filled moat, while the eighteenth-century Château de la Roche-aux-Moines is built in the most prestigious section of the vineyards, where the steep slopes overlook the river. Finally there are the elegant manor houses of Chamboureau and des Lauriers.

When the south-facing hills are too steep for machines to work the vines, horses are still used in some places.

Vouvray

LOIRE VALLEY

Vouvray is strung along the right bank of the Loire (*above*) at the beginning of vineyards that swathe the plateau in Chenin (*right*).

Balzac, the nineteenth-century novelist, was a connoisseur and a native of Tours who dreamed of one day owning the Château de Moncontour in Vouvray. The only thing missing was the money...

It is easy to understand why he wanted this particular château. It is on an ideal site, makes good wine, and is conveniently situated just on the outskirts of Tours. Here, just below Montcour, the Varennes spreads out level with Nozay and Vernou-sur-Brenne between the foot of the hillside and the right bank of the Loire. Then it suddenly draws back to let the Cisse – which has just merged with the Brenne – flow into the Loire. From this point on, the hills stand closer to the riverbank and actually overhang the Loire, which stretches out lazily between the little islands.

The village at the foot of the vines

The hills garland the edge of the slightly sloping limestone plateau as they run alongside the Loire beyond Tours toward Langeais. Only the long cleft slopes of the transverse valleys give access to the hills.

The village of Vouvray huddles at the foot of the hillside around its church, which was almost entirely rebuilt on Romanesque foundations during the nineteenth century. It is full of

Simply Chenin

Whether it is dry, medium, *moelleux*, *liquoreux*, *mousseux*, or *pétillant*, Vouvray can only be white, made solely as it is from Chenin Blanc. The appellation covers eight parishes, with Vouvray at the centre. There are various kinds of terroir above the calcareous foundation: sandy soils or *perruches*, clay-silica mixtures called *aubuis*, and chalky clay combinations. Depending on the way they face and the variations in the individual climates, these all do justice to Chenin's extraordinary plasticity. The wine has a marvellous natural acidity and can gain astonishing depths from Vendanges Tardives (the late-harvesting of wines) and botrytis rot. These contribute to its expressive aromas, dominated by acacia, lime, apple, and quince, evolving over the years towards mushroom, dried fruit, honey, and wax. The nuances of this wine are complex and infinite.

galleries that were hollowed out of the soft yellow tufa, either for building material or to create shelters, troglodyte dwellings, and chapels such as the one at Echeneau, which was converted in the sixteenth century. These galleries provide wonderful cellars, such as the famous Cave de la Bonne Dame, that maintain a constant cool temperature and are therefore ideal for Vouvray's wines.

Up on the plateau and on the surrounding slopes of the valleys, the vine reigns supreme. It rules over manors and châteaux often endowed with a wine-growing estate. To name a few, these include the Château de Moncontour, dating

mostly from the fifteenth century; the Manoir de la Gaudrelle, with its troglodyte wine cellars and converted eighteenth-century chapel; and the Manoir du Haut-Lieu, an eighteenth-century building set amid superb vines.

The houses with their superb cellars continue along the foot of the *côte* to the nearby village of Rochecorbon. The exceptional Romanesque church in this village, along with the semi-troglodyte, eleventh-century church in the hamlet of St-Georges, are reminders of the importance these places held through history – places with a wine-growing reputation which, for a long time, has been equal to that of Vouvray.

St-Pourçain-sur-Sioule

CENTRE

By the banks of the Sioule, the vineyards of St-Pourçain are dotted with villages whose châteaux and chapels reflect Bourbonnais's prestigious past (*right*).

From its source in the Puy-de-Dôme, the Sioule descends through gorges and makes its way to the Allier. As it meanders along the fringes of the Bourbonnais and Limagne areas, it traces a line between the old Pays d'Oc and the Pays d'Oïl. On the left bank of the river and the edges of a small tributary called the Bouble, the undulating countryside is dotted with limestone outcrops.

The area around St-Pourçain has an excellent reputation for viticulture, stretching back to the thirteenth-century when the Bourbonnais area became one of the main fiefs of France. In the fourteenth and fifteenth centuries, this reputation was rivalled only by that of the wine from Beaune. This fact tends to be forgotten today.

Peaceful Bourbonnais

St-Pourçain is sited between two bends in the river Sioule. The tranquil village centres around the immense, unusual Church of Ste Croix, a marriage of Romanesque and Gothic styles, built from the eleventh to the fifteenth centuries.

From the walls of the asymmetric building which are attached to the surrounding houses, the belfry of the former monastery emerges. Its towering height is a reminder that the town has played a key role throughout the centuries on account of its advantageous position on the Loire river route leading to the capital.

The Musée de la Vigne et du Terroir, beautifully located in the fifteenth-century Maison du Bailli (Baliff's House), recreates the viticultural traditions of the area and displays the wealth of its popular arts and crafts.

From the town gates, the fields, meadows, and vines present a tranquil rural mosaic which extends south towards Chantelle on the hilly banks of the Bouble. The countryside then runs north along the Sioule, and continues along the Allier in the direction of Moulins as far as Chemilly.

It is a land of Romanesque chapels and churches, pigeon houses, and hilltop châteaux. Next to St-Pourçain, a slender spire of a Romanesque church signals the village of Saulcet, which without doubt contains the best soils of the area. Also nearby, Verneuil-en-Bourbonnais has retained its medieval appearance. The village is notable for its solid twelfth-century collegiate Church of St Pierre, endowed with a powerful bell tower two centuries later.

Downstream on the Allier, Châtel-de-Neuvre stands in an exceptional location above the valley and possesses one of the finest Romanesque churches in the area, which, although of modest proportions, is the ultimate example of rural Bourbonnais architecture.

An invigorated appellation

Today, St-Pourçain's vineyard has been reduced to less than a tenth (about 600 hectares) of its former size. Having sat on royal tables in the past, its wine is now more suited to the common man. Based on the Gamay grape, the reds are fruity, supple, and of variable liveliness depending on how much Pinot Noir they contain. The white wines still use Tressalier, a traditional grape from this area, although Chardonnay and sometimes Sauvignon are the main varieties. These simple wines, labelled VDQS, are extremely pleasing to the palate, showing notes of their terroir that has contributed to renewed interest and might aspire to them being accorded AC status in the near future.

Sancerre

CENTRE

The vineyards of Sancerre are divided between the Sauvignon Blanc and Pinot Noir grape varieties.

On its long journey down to the Atlantic, the Loire runs along the eastern boundary of the Berry region. Not the pastoral Berry described by authors such as George Sand and Alain Fournier, but the Berry which lies around wine-producing Sancerre. Above the majestic course of the river, which is punctuated with small islands of sand and willows, the countryside is

Sancerre and its terroirs

Of the 2,500 wine-producing hectares of Sancerre, eighty per cent are planted with Sauvignon and twenty per cent with Pinot Noir. Sauvignon, the dominant white grape variety, is well-suited to the land that boasts an AC created in 1936 and widened in 1959 to include red and rosé wines. Areas known as the *terres blanches* (white soils) with their chalky limestone-clay base, produce robust wines that need a little time to reach their best – two to five years. Those of the calcareous *caillottes* (pebbles) give a fruity and aromatic palate to the youngest wine, while the *silex* (flint stones) ground produces wines that are full-flavoured but quite harsh before they evolve a degree of elegance. The distinctive vegetable and mineral traits of the fruit are common to all of these wines. Sancerre has no labelled *crus* but a number of the better terroirs in established localities have gained a confirmed reputation: for example, the Monts Damnés on the *terres blanches* of Chavignol; the Chêne Marchand on the *caillottes* of Bué; and the Romains on the *silex* soils of Sancerre. Strongly scented, dry, and – depending on the wine – either acidic or soft, Sancerre wine has known considerable success since World War II and particularly since the 1970s.

suddenly interrupted by steep hills, culminating in Sancerre's "peak". The slopes, at times extremely steep, are covered in vines. The crests of the hills are crowned with trees, and those parts that are less suited to viticulture are left to be grazed by the goats that produce the famous local cheese, Crottin de Chavignol. The level land at the bottom of the hills is allotted to meadows, and the small valleys to the scattered villages of the appellation.

A proud town

Peaceful and proud, Sancerre bathes in the gentle light of the Loire Valley, 306 metres (1,004 feet) above sea level and about 150 metres (490 feet) above the Loire. The small and tightly packed streets of the village bear nostalgic names such as rue du Carroir-de-Velours ("of the Velvet Square"), rue des Trois-Piliers ("of the Three Pillars"), rue des Pressoirs ("of Presses"). The houses are roofed in tiles and, more recently, slate, and also recall the past; in the rue du Carroir-de-Velours sits the haberdashery of Jacques Cœur's grandson, while at the end of the rue des Juifs is Charles V's salt storehouse for the salt tax. Overlooking the roofs of the town, the belfry (built in 1509) symbolizes the growing power of the sixteenth-century townspeople. Higher still, the late fourteenth-century Tour des Fiefs is the last remaining vestige of the ancient

The highest point in the village of Sancerre offers views over a valley devoted to viticulture.

Sancerre (*above*) overlooks its vineyards from a peak, topped by a belfry (to the left) and the Tour de Fiefs (to the right). At the foot of the village, bordering the canal, stands Ménétréol-sous-Sancerre (*right*).

château of the Counts of Sancerre. From the top of its ninety-five steps is a marvellous, uninterrupted view over the Loire Valley and its vineyards. Other points for viewing superb panoramas are the Porte César gate and along the ramparts surrounding the town: Remparts des Augustins, Remparts des Abreuvoirs, and Remparts des Dames.

One name, one wine

"Wine comprises the principle industry and the main commercial activity in this area, which owns several vintages of full-bodied wines with plenty of bouquet," noted the writer Balzac in 1843, in *La Muse du Département*. Indeed, the town owes most of its wealth to its vineyards. Their development during the eleventh and twelfth centuries went hand in hand with the growing power of the Counts of Sancerre – a title created in 1152 when the lands of the House of Blois-Champagne were split between the sons of Count Thibaud IV.

Sancerre was planted with Pinot Noir vines from Burgundy and gained a good reputation for red wines that would last until Balzac's day. When phylloxera hit at the end of the nineteenth century, however, and the vineyards had to be replanted, the Sauvignon variety gained the upper hand. So it is for white wines that we know the terroirs of Sancerre and its charming wine-growing villages, from Chavignol (highly renowned since ancient times), Amigny, and Bué, to Verdigny, Sury-en-Vaux, and Crézancy.

Glossary

AOC

See Guarantee or indication of origin

AROMA

Characteristic bouquet or fragrance of the wine.

BLENDING

See Cuvée

BOTRYTIS CINEREA

See Noble rot

CLOS

An enclosed or walled vineyard.

CRU

This word means "single vineyard". In the broader sense it refers to a region of excellence or to the wine that comes from that region. For example, *grand cru* is a term used to indicate an extraordinary wine. In Burgundy and Alsace the term is used as an official classification for the best wine-growing areas.

CUVÉE

There is no exact definition for this term, which its most basic level means 'vat'. In general it is used to describe the high-quality wine blend that comes from different grapes, regions and vintages and makes the final wine product: the *assemblage* (mixture). It is used in particular in the production of sparkling wines and Champagne.

FERMENTATION

A spontaneous fermentation occurs when yeast fungi comes into contact with watery sugar solutions at a temperature between 18° and 27°C (64° and 81°F). Until the nineteenth century, fermentation was regarded as a natural process of decay. Louis Pasteur

discovered that micro-organisms are involved in the process in 1857. In wine production, fermentation describes the process by which sugar in the must is transformed into alcohol and carbon dioxide by adding wine yeast.

GUARANTEE OR INDICATION OF ORIGIN

In France, official indications of origin and classification are given by the Institut National des Appellations d´Origine (INAO). French wines conform to four different categories, which must, by law, appear on the label:
1. AC (*appellation contrôlée*): This is the strictest classification. The variety of grapes used, the processing methods, and the quantity produced are meticulously controlled. The method of control varies from region to region. Every region follows its own rules. For example, in the best wine producing areas of Burgundy, every *côte* (slope or hillside) has its own appellation, while the Champagne appellation, on the other hand, includes the whole region as well as the method of production.
2. VDQS (*vin délimité de qualité supérieure*): These are wines of higher quality that come from specific growing areas. They go through a control that is as rigorous as that of the ACs.
3. *Vin de pays*: These "country wines" are not allowed to be blended. The region that they come from appears on the label. They have to meet higher quality standards than table wines.
4. *Vin de table*: Table wines can be blended from wines of different growing areas. The label gives the brand name and the degrees of alcohol the wine contains.

NOBLE ROT

This process is caused by the *Botrytis cinerea* fungus. A temperate climate and humid weather offer beneficial conditions for its development. When the fungus attacks ripe and normally healthy grapes, they shrink, becoming grey at first, and then finally brown. During this process the grapes lose half their weight but less than half of their sugar content. Their highly concentrated juice generates high-quality, sweet wines. There is a fine line, however, between success and failure, for if this type of fungus were to attack unripe or half-ripe grapes whose sugar content is less than 70 per cent of the weight of must, it would turn into one of the most dangerous diseases in the vineyard, ruining the grapes.

RACKING

The process of transferring clear wine into an empty container in order to remove it from undesirable sediments that lie on the bottom.

TANNING AGENT

See Tannin

TANNIN

Tannins are found naturally in many trees and fruits, and have been used in leather processing as tanning agents for millennia. Numerous red grape varieties, in particular, contain various tannins in their skin. Tannins play an important role in the ageing process, allowing certain red wines to be kept for longer. In the course of maturation the tannin content becomes milder, but it is especially noticeable in young wines. Tannin has an astringent effect, which means it causes a furry sensation on the tongue.

TERROIR

In its narrow sense, terroir means a soil that is especially suited for wine-growing. Since the 1920s, the term has been used in a much broader manner, to denote all of the natural conditions of the vineyard. A terroir gives its wine a special and distinctive character. The interaction of many elements plays a decisive role in the evolution of that character: the climate, the condition of the soil, the landscape, the temperatures during the day and night, distribution of precipitation (rainfall), water drainage, the way the slope faces, the number of hours and type of sunshine it gets, the type of cultivation used, etc. These factors have an influence on the biology of the vine and therefore affect the actual consistency of the grape. The specific aroma that the grape develops from these conditions is called the *goût du terroir* (terroir flavour).

VDN *(vins doux naturels)*

These are naturally sweet, fortified wines; the sweetness is the "natural" part of the title – not the alcoholic strength. They are made by adding highly concentrated alcohol to a sweet wine must of specific grape varieties, which contains at least 125g (4oz) residual sugar. They are all made from VDN or AC wines and contain between 15 and 16 degrees of alcohol.

VDQS

See Guarantee or indication of origin

Addresses

ANCENIS

(Loire Valley) – page 140
Principal appellations
produced in the commune:
Muscadet Coteaux de la Loire;
Coteaux d'Ancenis
Tourist Information:
Office du Tourisme
27 rue du Château
44150 Ancenis
Tel/Fax: 00 33 (0)2 40 83 07 44
Syndicat viticole:
Syndicat des Coteaux d'Ancenis
Le Pré Hausse
44150 St-Géréon
Cave coopérative viticole:
Les Vignerons de la Noëlle
Blvd des Alliers - BP 155
44154 Ancenis
Tel: 00 33 (0)2 40 98 92 72
Fax: 00 33 (0)2 40 98 96 70

ARBIN

(Savoie) – page 52
Principal appellations
produced in the commune:
Vin de Savoie Arbin,
Vin de Savoie
Tourist Information:
Mairie/Office du Tourisme
Grand-rue
73800 Arbin
Tel: 00 33 (0)4 79 84 09 25
Fax: 00 33 (0)4 79 84 34 45
Syndicat viticole:
Comité Interprofessionnel
des Vins de Savoie
3 rue du Château
73000 Chambéry
Tel: 00 33 (0)4 79 33 44 16
Fax: 00 33 (0)4 79 85 92 47

ARBOIS

(Jura) – page 46
Principal appellations
produced in the commune:
Arbois; Côtes du Jura; Arbois Vin
Jaune; Arbois Vin de Paille;
Crémant du Jura
Tourist Information:
Office du Tourisme
10 rue de l'Hôtel-de-Ville
39600 Arbois
Tel: 00 33 (0)3 84 66 55 50
Syndicat viticole:
Comité Interprofessionnel
des Vins d'AOC du Jura
Château Pecauld
BP 41 - 39602 Arbois Cedex
Tel: 00 33 (0)3 84 66 26 14
Fax: 00 33 (0)3 84 66 10 29
E-mail: civg@jura-vins.com
Caves coopératives viticoles:
- Fruitière Vinicole d'Arbois
Château Béthanie
2 rue des Fossés

39600 Arbois
Tel: 00 33 (0)3 84 66 11 67
Fax: 00 33 (0)3 84 37 48 80
- Les Ambassadeurs des Vins jaunes
Château Pecauld - BP 41
39600 Arbois
Tel: 00 33 (0)3 84 66 26 14
E-mail: percee@jura-vins.com
Museum:
Musée de la Vigne et du Vin
Château Pecauld
39600 Arbois
Tel: 00 33 (0)3 84 66 40 45
Fax: 00 33 (0)3 84 6640 46

AY

(Champagne) – page 10
Principal appellations
produced in the commune:
Champagne; Coteaux Champenois
Tourist Information:
Mairie/Office du Tourisme:
1 Place Henri -Martin
51160 Ay
Tel: 00 33 (0)3 26 56 92 10
Fax: 00 33 (0)3 26 54 84 76
Syndicats viticoles:
- Comité Interprofessionnel
du Vin de Champagne
5 rue Henri-Martin - BP 135
51204 Epernay Cedex
Tel: 00 33 (0)3 26 51 19 30
Fax: 00 33 (0)3 26 51 26 20
Internet site: www.champagne.fr
- Syndicat Général des Vignerons
de la Champagne:
44 Av. Jean-Jaurès - BP 176
51200 Epernay
Tel: 00 33 (0)3 26 51 19 30
Fax: 00 33 (0)3 26 51 26 20
Internet site: www.champagne-
vignerons.fr
- Union des Maisons de Champagne
1 rue Marie-Stuart – BP 2185
51081 Reims Cedex
Tel: 00 33 (0)3 26 47 26 89
Fax: 00 33 (0)3 26 47 48 44
Internet site: http://www.umc.fr
Cave coopérative viticole:
Champagne Raoul Collet
14 Blvd Pasteur
51160 Ay
Tel: 00 33 (0)3 26 55 15 88
Fax: 00 33 (0)3 26 54 02 40

AZAY-LE-RIDEAU

(Loire Valley) – page 142
Principal appellations
produced in the commune:
Touraine Azay-le-Rideau; Touraine
Tourist Information:
Office du Tourisme
4 rue du Château - BP 5
37190 Azay-le-Rideau
Tel: 00 33 (0)2 47 45 44 40
Fax: 00 33 (0)2 47 45 31 46

BANYULS

(Roussillon) – page 104
Principal appellations
produced in the commune:
Banyuls; Collioure;
Muscat de Rivesaltes
Tourist Information:
Office du Tourisme
Avenue de la République
66650 Banyuls-sur-Mer
Tel: 00 33 (0)4 68 88 31 58
Fax: 00 33 (0)4 68 88 36 84
Syndicat viticole:
Syndicat du Cru Banyuls
Mas Reig
66650 Banyuls-sur-Mer
Tel: 00 33 (0)4 68 88 72 92
Fax: 00 33 (0)4 68 88 72 94
E-mail: cru.banuyls@wanadoo.fr
Caves coopératives viticoles:
- Cave Coopérative de l'Etoile
26 Avenue du Puig-Del-Mas
BP 32 - 66650 Banyuls-sur-Mer
Tel: 00 33 (0)4 68 88 00 10
Fax: 00 33 (0)4 68 88 15 10
- Cave de l'abbé Rous
56 Avenue Charles-de-Gaulle
66650 Banyuls-sur-Mer
Tel: 00 33 (0)4 68 88 72 72
Fax: 00 33 (0)0 33 (0)4 68 88 30 57
- Cave du Cellier des Templiers
rue du Mas-Reig
66652 Banyuls-sur-Mer
Tel: 00 33 (0)4 68 98 36 70
Fax: 00 33 (0)4 68 98 36 91

BAUX-DE-PROVENCE [LES]

(Provence) – page 72
Principal appellation
produced in the commune:
Les Baux-de-Provence
Tourist Information:
Office du Tourisme
Maison du Roy
rue Porte-Mage
13520 Les Baux-de-Provence
Tel: 00 33 (0)4 90 54 34 39
Fax: 00 33 (0)4 90 54 51 15
Syndicat viticole:
Syndicat des Baux-de-Provence
Estoublon - 13990 Fontvieille
Tel: 00 33 (0)4 90 54 64 00

BEAUNE

(Burgundy) – page 24
Principal appellations
produced in the commune:
Beaune; Beaune Premier Cru;
Côte de Beaune;
Hautes Côtes de Beaune
Tourist Information:
- Office du Tourisme
1 rue de l'Hôtel-Dieu
21203 Beaune
Tel: 00 33 (0)3 80 26 21 30
Fax: 00 33 (0)3 80 26 21 39

- Syndicat Touristique des Hautes-Côtes
Avenue du 8-Septembre
21200 Beaune
Tel: 00 33 (0)3 80 24 20 75
Fax: 00 33 (0)3 80 24 03 88
E-mail: www.cotedor-tourisme.com
Syndicat viticole:
Bureau Interprofessionnel
des Vins de Bourgogne
12 Blvd Bretonnière - BP 150
21204 Beaune Cedex
Tel: 00 33 (0)3 80 25 04 80
Fax: 00 33 (0)3 80 25 04 81
E-mail: bivb@wanadoo.fr
Cave coopérative viticole:
Les Caves des Hautes-Côtes
Route de Pommard - 21200 Beaune
Tel: 00 33 (0)3 80 25 01 00
Fax: 00 33 (0)3 80 22 87 05
Museum:
Musée du Vin de Bourgogne
Palais des Ducs de Bourgogne
rue de l'Enfer - 21200 Beaune
Tel: 00 33 (0)3 80 22 08 19

BERGERAC

(Southwest) – page 112
Principal appellations
Produced in the commune:
Bergerac, Côtes de Bergerac,
Pécharmant, Rosette
Tourist Information:
Office du Tourisme
97 rue Neuve-d'Argenson
24100 Bergerac
Tel: 00 33 (0)5 53 57 03 11
Fax: 00 33 (0)5 53 61 11 04
Syndicat viticole:
Conseil Interprofessionnel
des Vins de la Région de Bergerac
1 rue des Récollets
24104 Bergerac Cedex
Tel: 00 33 (0)5 53 63 57 57
Fax: 00 33 (0)5 53 63 01 30
Cave coopérative viticole:
Union Vinicole Bergerac Le Fleix
24130 Le Fleix
Tel: 00 33 (0)5 53 24 64 32
Fax: 00 33 (0)5 53 24 65 46
Museum:
Musée du Vin et de la Batellerie
5 rue des Conférences
24100 Bergerac
Tel: 00 33 (0)5 53 57 80 92

BLAYE

(Bordeaux) – page 126
Principal appellations
produced in the commune:
Blaye; Côtes de Blaye;
Premières Côtes de Blaye
Tourist Information:
Office du Tourisme
2 Allées Marines - 33390 Blaye
Tel: 00 33 (0)5 57 42 12 09
Fax: 00 33 (0)5 57 42 91 94

Syndicats viticoles:
- Conseil Interprofessionnel
des Vins de Bordeaux
1 Cours du 30-Juillet
33075 Bordeaux Cedex
Tel: 00 33 (0)0 33 (0)5 56 00 22 66
Fax: 00 33 (0)5 56 00 22 77
E-mail: civb@vins-bordeaux.fr
- Syndicat Viticole et Maison du Vin
des Côtes de Blaye:
11 Cours Vauban
33390 Blaye
Tel: 00 33 (0)5 57 42 91 19
Fax: 00 33 (0)5 57 42 85 28
Cave coopérative viticole:
Union des Producteurs de Blaye
Le Piquet
33390 Cars
Tel: 00 33 (0)5 57 42 13 15
Fax: 00 33 (0)5 57 42 84 92

BONNIEUX
(Provence) – page 76
Principal appellation
produced in the commune:
Côtes du Lubéron
Tourist Information:
Office du Tourisme
7 Place Carnot
84480 Bonnieux
Tel: 00 33 (0)4 90 75 91 90
Point Phone: 04 90 75 92 94
Cave coopérative viticole:
Cave de Bonnieux
Quartier de la Gare
84480 Bonnieux
Tel: 04 90 75 80 03
Fax: 00 33 (0)4 90 75 98 30

BRIGNOLES
(Provence) – page 80
Principal appellations
produced in the commune:
Coteaux Varois; Côtes de Provence
Tourist Information:
Office du Tourisme
10 rue du Palais
83170 Brignoles
Tel: 04 94 69 27 51
Fax: 00 33 (0)4 94 69 44 08
Syndicats viticoles:
- Syndicat des Vignerons du Var
83170 Brignoles
Tel: 00 33 (0)4 94 59 13 58
Fax: 00 33 (0)4 94 59 25 20
- Maison des vins coteaux Varois
Abbaye de La Celle - 83170 La Celle
Tel: 00 33 (0)4 94 69 33 18
Fax: 00 33 (0)4 94 59 04 47

CAHORS
(Southwest) – page 116
Principal appellations
produced in the commune:
Cahors
Tourist Information:
Office du Tourisme
Place François-Mitterrand
46000 Cahors
Tel: 00 33 (0)5 65 53 20 65
Fax: 00 33 (0)5 65 53 20 74

Syndicat viticole:
Union Interprofessionnelle
du Vin de Cahors
430 Avenue Jean-Jaurès
46002 Cahors Cedex
Tel: 00 33 (0)5 65 23 22 24
Fax: 00 33 (0)5 65 23 22 27
Cave coopérative viticole:
Caves des Côtes d'Olt
46140 Parnac
Tel: 00 33 (0)5 65 30 71 86
Fax: 00 33 (0)5 65 30 35 28

CASSIS
(Provence) – page 82
Principal appellations
produced in the commune:
Cassis
Tourist Information:
Office du Tourisme
Quai des Moulins
13260 Cassis
Fax: 00 33 (0)4 42 01 28 31
E-mail: omt@cassis.fr
Syndicat viticole:
Syndicat des Vignerons de Cassis
Château de Fontcreuse
Route de la Ciotat
13260 Cassis
Tel: 00 33 (0)4 42 01 71 09
Fax: 00 33 (0)4 42 01 28 31

CERDON
(Bugey) – page 50
Principal appellations
produced in the commune:
Vin du Bugey Cerdon; Vin du Bugey
Tourist Information:
Office du Tourisme
Place Allombert
01450 Cerdon
Tel: 00 33 (0)4 74 39 93 02
Syndicat viticole:
Syndicat des vins du Bugey
Av. du 133e Régiment-d'Infanterie
01300 Belley
Tel: 00 33 (0)4 79 81 30 17
Fax: 00 33 (0)4 79 81 55 10

CHABLIS
(Burgundy) – page 28
Principal appellations
produced in the commune:
Petit Chablis; Chablis;
Chablis Premier Cru;
Chablis Grand Cru
Tourist Information:
Office du Tourisme
1 rue du Maréchal de Lattre de
Tassigny - 89800 Chablis
Tel: 00 33 (0)3 86 42 80 80
Fax: 00 33 (0)3 86 42 49 71
Syndicat viticole:
Bureau Interprofessionnel des Vins
de Bourgogne (Chablis/Auxerrois)
Le Petit Pontigny
1 rue de Chichée BP - 31
89800 Chablis Cedex
Tel: 00 33 (0)3 86 42 42 22
Fax: 00 33 (0)3 86 42 80 16
E-mail: bivb.Chablis@bivb.com

Cave coopérative viticole:
La Chablisienne
8 Blvd Pasteur - BP 14
89800 Chablis
Tel: 00 33 (0)3 86 42 89 89
Fax: 00 33 (0)3 86 42 89 90

CHATEAU-CHALON
(Jura) – page 48
Principal appellations
produced in the commune:
Château-Chalon; Côtes du Jura
Tourist Information:
Mairie/Office du Tourisme:
rue St Jean - 39210 Château-Chalon
Tel: 00 33 (0)3 84 44 62 90

CHATEAUNEUF-DU-PAPE
(Rhône Valley) – page 56
Principal appellations
produced in the commune:
Châteauneuf-du-Pape;
Côtes du Rhône
Tourist Information:
Office du Tourisme
Place du Portail
84230 Châteauneuf-du-Pape
Tel: 00 33 (0)4 90 83 71 08
Fax: 00 33 (0)4 90 83 50 34
E-mail: tourisme-chato9-
pape@wanadoo.fr
Syndicats viticoles:
- Fédération de Producteurs
de Châteauneuf-du-Pape
12 Avenue Pasteur - BP 12
84231 Châteauneuf-du-Pape Cedex
Tel: 00 33 (0)4 90 83 72 21
Fax: 00 33 (0)4 90 83 70 01
Internet site: www.chateauneuf.com
- SIDVAOC (Syndicat Intercommunal
de Défense Viticole de l'appellation
d'Origine Contrôlée)
Institut Rhodanien
2260 Route du Grès - 84100 Orange
Tel: 00 33 (0)4 90 11 46 23
Fax: 00 33 (0)4 90 11 46 24
Maison des Vins:
Vinadéa
8, rue Maréchal-Foch
84232 Châteauneuf-du-Pape
Tel/Fax: 00 33 (0)4 90 83 70 69
Internet site: www.vinadea.com
Museum:
Musée du Vin
Route d'Avignon
84231 Châteauneuf-du-Pape
Tel: 00 33 (0)4 90 83 70 07
Fax: 00 33 (0)4 90 83 74 34
E-mail: musee@brotte.com

CHEVERNY
(Loire Valley) – page 144
Principal appellations
produced in the commune:
Cheverny; Cour-Cheverny; Touraine
Tourist Information:
Office du Tourisme
12 rue Chêne-des-Dames
41700 Cheverny
Tel: 00 33 (0)2 54 79 95 63
Fax: 00 33 (0)2 54 79 23 90

CHIGNIN
(Savoie) – page 54
Principal appellations
produced in the commune:
Vin de Savoie Chignin;
Vin de Savoie Chignin-Bergeron;
Vin de Savoie
Tourist Information:
Mairie/Office du Tourisme:
Chef Lieu
73800 Chignin
Tel: 00 33 (0)4 79 28 10 12
Fax: 00 33 (0)4 79 28 01 36
Syndicat viticole:
Comité Interprofessionnel
des Vins de Savoie
3 rue du Château
73000 Chambéry
Tel: 00 33 (0)4 79 33 44 16
Fax: 00 33 (0)4 79 85 92 47

CHINON
(Loire Valley) – page 146
Principal appellation
produced in the commune:
Chinon
Tourist Information:
Office du Tourisme
Place Hofheim
37500 Chinon
Tel: 00 33 (0)2 47 93 17 85
Fax: 00 33 (0)2 47 93 93 05
Museum:
Musée Animé du Vin
et de la Tonnellerie
12 rue Voltaire
37500 Chinon
Tel: 00 33 (0)2 47 93 25 63

COLLIOURE
(Roussillon) – page 108
Principal appellation
produced in the commune:
Collioure; Banyuls;
Muscat de Rivesaltes
Tourist Information:
Office du Tourisme
Place du 18-Juin
66190 Collioure
Tel: 00 33 (0)4 68 82 15 47
Fax: 00 33 (0)4 68 82 46 29
Syndicat viticole:
Syndicat du cru Collioure
Mas Reig
66650 Banyuls-sur-Mer
Tel: 00 33 (0)4 68 88 72 92
Fax: 00 33 (0)4 68 88 72 94
E-mail: cru.banyuls@wanadoo.fr
Cave coopérative viticole:
Le Cellier des Dominicains
Place Orphila
66190 Collioure
Tel: 00 33 (0)4 68 82 05 63
Fax: 00 33 (0)4 68 82 43 06
E-mail: le-dominicain@wanadoo.fr

CONDRIEU
(Rhône Valley) – page 60
Principal appellations
produced in the commune:
Condrieu; Côtes du Rhône

Tourist Information:
Office du Tourisme
Place du Séquoia
69420 Condrieu
Tel: 00 33 (0)4 74 56 62 83
Fax: 00 33 (0)4 74 56 65 85
E-mail: otcondrieu@wanadoo.fr

EGUISHEIM
(Alsace) – page 16
Principal appellations
produced in the commune:
Alsace Grand Cru Eichberg;
Alsace Grand Cru Pfersigberg;
Alsace Riesling; Alsace
Gewurztraminer;
Alsace Tokay-Pinot Gris;
Alsace Pinot Noir; Alsace Muscat
Tourist Information:
Office du Tourisme
22A Grande rue
68420 Eguisheim
Tel: 00 33 (0)3 89 23 40 33
Fax: 00 33 (0)3 89 41 86 20
Internet site: www.ot-eguisheim.fr
Syndicats viticoles:
- Conseil Interprofessionnel
des Vins d'Alsace
Maison des Vins d'Alsace
12 Av. de la Foire-aux-Vins
68012 Colmar Cedex
Tel: 00 33 (0)3 89 20 16 20
Fax: 00 33 (0)3 89 20 16 30
- Syndicat des Vignerons
Récoltants d'Alsace
rue Jean-Mermoz
68015 Colmar Cedex
Tel: 00 33 (0)3 89 41 97 41
Fax: 00 33 (0)3 89 23 01 97
E-mail: virginie@civa.fr
Cave coopérative viticole:
Cave Vinicole Wolfberger
6 Grande-rue
68420 Eguisheim
Tel: 00 33 (0)3 89 22 20 20
Fax: 00 33 (0)3 89 23 47 09

FRONSAC
(Bordeaux) – page 128
Principal appellations
produced in the commune:
Fronsac; Canon-Fronsac
Tourist Information:
Mairie/Office du Tourisme:
8 rue Général-de-Gaulle
33126 Fronsac
Tel: 00 33 (0)5 57 51 30 20
Fax: 00 33 (0)5 57 51 60 35
Syndicats viticoles:
- Conseil Interprofessionnel
des Vins de Bordeaux
1 Cours du 30-Juillet
33075 Bordeaux Cedex
Tel: 00 33 (0)5 56 00 22 66
Fax: 00 33 (0)5 56 00 22 77
E-mail: civb@vins-bordeaux.fr
- Syndicat Viticole et Maison du Vin
de Fronsac et Canon-Fronsac
Plaisance - 33126 Fronsac
Tel: 00 33 (0)5 57 51 80 51
Fax: 00 33 (0)5 57 25 98 19

GAILLAC
(Southwest) – page 118
Principal appellations
produced in the commune:
Gaillac; Premières Côtes de Gaillac
Tourist Information:
Office du Tourisme
Abbaye St-Michel - 81600 Gaillac
Tel: 00 33 (0)5 63 57 14 65
Fax: 00 33 (0)5 63 57 61 37
Syndicat viticole:
Comité Interprofessionnel
des Vins de Gaillac
Maison de la Vigne et du Vin
81600 Gaillac
Tel: 00 33 (0)5 63 57 15 40
Fax: 00 33 (0)5 63 57 20 01
E-mail: civg@vins-gaillac.com

GIGONDAS
(Rhône Valley) – page 62
Principal appellations
produced in the commune:
Gigondas; Côtes du Rhône
Tourist Information:
Office du Tourisme
Place du Portail - 84190 Gigondas
Tel: 00 33 (0)4 90 65 85 46
Fax: 00 33 (0)4 90 65 88 42
Cave coopérative viticole:
Cave des Vignerons de Gigondas
84190 Gigondas
Tel: 00 33 (0)4 90 65 86 27
Fax: 00 33 (0)4 90 65 80 13

GRIGNAN
(Rhône Valley) – page 66
Principal appellation
produced in the commune:
Coteaux du Tricastin
Tourist Information:
Office du Tourisme
Chef-lieu du Canton
Place du Jeu du Ballon
26230 Grignan
Tel: 00 33 (0)4 75 46 56 75
Fax: 00 33 (0)4 75 46 55 89
Syndicat viticole:
Syndicat des Vignerons
des Coteaux du Tricastin
Grande rue - 26230 Grignan
Tel: 00 33 (0)4 75 46 55 96
Fax: 00 33 (0)4 75 46 56 05

HAUTVILLERS
(Champagne) – page 12
Principal appellations
produced in the commune:
Champagne; Coteaux Champenois
Tourist Information:
Office du Tourisme
Place de la Republique
51160 Hautvillers
Tel: 00 33 (0)3 26 57 06 35
Fax: 00 33 (0)3 26 51 72 66
Syndicat viticole:
- Comité Interprofessionnel
du Vin de Champagne
5 rue Henri-Martin - BP 135
51200 Epernay Cedex
Tel: 00 33 (0)3 26 54 47 20

Fax: 00 33 (0)3 26 55 49 79
Internet site: www.champagne.fr
- Syndicat Général des Vignerons
de la Champagne
44 Av. Jean-Jaurès - BP 176
51205 Epernay Cedex
Tel: 00 33 (0)3 26 59 55 00
Fax: 00 33 (0)3 26 54 97 27
Internet site:
www.champagne-vignerons.fr
- Union des Maisons de Champagne
1 rue Marie-Stuart - 51081 Reims
Tel: 00 33 (0)3 26 47 26 89
Fax: 00 33 (0)3 26 47 48 44
Internet site: http://www.umc.fr
Museum:
Musée de l'abbaye d'Hautvillers
rue de Cumières - 51160 Hautvillers
(Moët et Chandon, visits by
appointment)
Tel: 00 33 (0)3 26 51 20 00

IRANCY
(Burgundy) – page 30
Principal appellation
produced in the commune:
Irancy
Tourist Information:
Mairie/Office du Tourisme:
89290 Irancy
Syndicat viticole:
Bureau Interprofessionnel des Vins
de Bourgogne (Chablis/Auxerrois)
Le Petit Pontigny
1 rue de Chichée BP31
89800 Chablis
Tel: 00 33 (0)3 86 42 42 22
Fax: 00 33 (0)3 86 42 80 16
E-mail: bivb@wanadoo.fr

IROULEGUY
(Southwest) – page 122
Principal appellation
produced in the commune:
Irouléguy
Tourist Information:
Mairie/Office du Tourisme:
64220 Irouléguy
Tel: 00 33 (0)5 59 37 17 96
Syndicat viticole:
Syndicat des Vignerons AOC
Irouléguy
64430 Irouléguy
Tel: 00 33 (0)5 59 37 41 33
Fax: 00 33 (0)5 59 37 47 76
Cave coopérative viticole:
Les Maîtres Vignerons d'Irouléguy
Route de St-Jean-Pied-de-Port
64430 St-Etienne-de-Baïgorry
Tel: 00 33 (0)5 59 37 41 33
Fax: 00 33 (0)5 59 37 47 76

KIENTZHEIM
(Alsace) – page 18
Principal appellations
produced in the commune:
Alsace Grand Cru Schlossberg;
Alsace Grand Cru Furstentum;
Alsace Riesling; Alsace
Gewurztraminer; Alsace Tokay-Pinot
Gris; Alsace Pinot Noir; Alsace Muscat

Tourist Information:
Mairie/Office du Tourisme:
13, Grand'rue
68240 Kientzheim
Tel: 00 33 (0)3 89 47 12 62
Fax: 00 33 (0)3 89 78 14 65
Syndicats viticoles:
- Syndicat des Vignerons Récoltants
d'Alsace
rue Jean-Mermoz
68015 Colmar Cedex
Tel: 00 33 (0)3 89 41 97 41
Fax: 00 33 (0)3 89 23 01 97
- Conseil Interprofessionnel
des Vins d'Alsace
Maison des Vins d'Alsace
12 Av. de la Foire-aux-Vins
68012 Colmar Cedex
Tel: 00 33 (0)3 89 20 16 20
Fax: 00 33 (0)3 89 20 16 30
Internet site: www.vinalsace.com
Cave coopérative viticole:
Cave de Kientzheim-Kaysersberg
10 rue des Vieux-Moulins
68240 Kientzheim
Tel: 00 33 (0)3 89 47 13 19
Fax: 00 33 (0)3 89 47 34 38
Museum:
Musée du Vignoble
et des Vins d'Alsace
Château - Confrérie St-Etienne
1 bis, Grand'rue
68240 Kientzheim
Tel: 00 33 (0)3 89 78 21 36

LAGRASSE
(Languedoc) – page 96
Principal appellation
produed in the commune:
Corbières
Tourist Information:
Office du Tourisme
6 Blvd de la Promenade
11220 Lagrasse
Tel: 00 33 (0)4 68 43 11 56
Fax: 00 33 (0)4 68 43 16 34
E-mail: info@lafrasse.com
Internet site: www.lagrasse.com

MADIRAN
(Southwest) – page 124
Principal appellations
produced in the commune:
Madiran, Pacherenc du Vic Bilh
Tourist Information:
Mairie/Office du Tourisme:
34 Route du Vignoble
65700 Madiran
Tel: 00 33 (0)5 62 31 98 09
Fax: 00 33 (0)5 62 31 90 09
Syndicat viticole:
Syndicat des Vignerons AOC
de Madiran
65700 Madiran
Tel: 00 33 (0)5 62 31 90 67
Fax: 00 33 (0)5 62 31 90 79
Cave coopérative viticole:
Les Vignerons du Vic Bilh Madiran
64350 Crouseilles
Tel: 00 33 (0)5 59 68 10 93
Fax: 00 33 (0)5 59 68 14 33

MARGAUX

(Bordeaux) – page 130

Principal appellations
produced in the commune:
Margaux; Haut Médoc; Bordeaux

Tourist Information:
Office du Tourisme
Maison du Vin et
du Tourisme de Margaux
Place de la Trémoille
33460 Margaux
Tel: 00 33 (0)5 57 88 70 82
Fax: 00 33 (0)5 57 88 38 27

Syndicats viticoles:
- Conseil Interprofessionnel
des Vins de Bordeaux
1 Cours du 30-Juillet
33075 Bordeaux Cedex
Tel: 00 33 (0)5 56 00 22 66
Fax: 00 33 (0)5 56 00 22 77
E-mail: civb@vins-bordeaux.fr
- Maison du Vin et du Tourisme
et Syndicat Viticole de Margaux
Place de la Tremoille
33460 Margaux
Tel: 00 33 (0)5 57 88 70 82
Fax: 00 33 (0)5 57 88 38 27

MENERBES

(Provence) – page 86

Principal appellation
produced in the commune:
Côtes du Lubéron

Tourist Information:
Mairie/Office du Tourisme:
Place de l'Horloge
84560 Ménerbes
Tel: 00 33 (0)4 90 72 22 05
Fax: 00 33 (0)4 90 72 48 13

Museum:
Musée du Tire-Bouchon
Route de Cavaillon
84560 Ménerbes
Tel: 00 33 (0)4 90 72 41 58
Fax: 00 33 (0)4 90 72 41 59

MINERVE

(Languedoc) – page 100

Principal appellation
produced in the commune:
Minervois

Tourist Information:
Mairie/Office du Tourisme:
2 rue des Remparts
34210 Minerve
Tel / Fax: 00 33 (0)4 68 91 22 92

Syndicat viticole:
Syndicat du Cru Minervois
Château de Siran
34210 Siran
Tel: 00 33 (0)4 68 27 80 00
Fax: 00 33 (0)4 68 27 80 01

MONTMARTRE

(Paris) – page 8

Principale appellation
produced in the commune:
Clos Montmartre (not for retail
sale, sold by auction in support
of the work of the commune
of Montmarte)

Tourist Information:
Office du Tourisme
Syndicat d'Initiative de Montmartre
21 Place du Tertre - 75018 Paris
Tel: 00 33 (0)1 42 62 21 21
Fax: 00 33 (0)1 42 62 60 68

OINGT

(Burgundy) – page 42

Principal appellations
produced in the commune:
Beaujolais; Beaujolais-Villages

Tourist Information:
Mairie/Office du Tourisme:
rue Paul-Causeret - 69620 Oingt
Tel: 00 33 (0)4 74 71 21 24
Fax: 00 33 (0)4 74 71 15 50

Syndicat viticole:
Inter Beaujolais
210 Blvd Vermorel
69400 Villefranche
Tel: 00 33 (0)4 74 02 22 10
Fax: 00 33 (0)4 74 02 22 19
E-mail:
interbeaujolais@beaujolais.net

Cave coopérative viticole:
Cave des Vignerons du Doury
69620 Le Bois-d'Oingt
Tel: 00 33 (0)4 74 71 30 52
Fax: 00 33 (0)4 74 71 35 28

PATRIMONIO

(Corsica) – page 94

Principal appellations
produced in the commune:
Patrimonio; Muscat du Cap Corse

Tourist Information:
Mairie /Office du Tourisme:
Le Village - 20253 Patrimonio
Tel: 00 33 (0)4 95 37 08 49
Fax: 00 33 (0)4 95 37 05 78

Syndicat viticole:
Comité Intersyndical
des Vins de Corse
Place St-Nicholas
7, Blvd du Général de Gaulle
20200 Bastia
Tel: 00 33 (0)4 95 32 91 32
Fax: 00 33 (0)4 95 32 87 81

PERNAND-VERGELESSES

(Burgundy) – page 34

Principal appellations
produced in the commune:
Pernand-Vergelesses;
Pernand-Vergelesses Premier Cru;
Corton; Corton-Charlemagne;

Tourist Information:
Mairie/Office du Tourisme:
Village de Pernand
21420 Pernand-Vergelesses
Tel: 00 33 (0)3 80 21 57 05
Fax: 00 33 (0)3 80 26 13 67

Syndicat viticole:
Bureau Interprofessionnel
des Vins de Bourgogne
12 Blvd Bretonnière
21204 Beaune Cedex
Tel: 00 33 (0)3 80 25 04 80
Fax: 00 33 (0)3 80 25 04 90
E-mail: bivb@wanadoo.fr

RICEYS [LES]

(Champagne) – page 14

Principal appellations
produced in the commune:
Rosé des Riceys; Champagne;
Coteaux Champenois

Tourist Information:
Office du Tourisme
14 Place des Héros-de-la-Résistance
10340 Les Riceys-Haut
Tel: 00 33 (0)3 25 29 15 38

Syndicats viticoles:
- Comité Interprofessionnel
du Vin de Champagne
5 rue Henri-Martin - BP 135
51204 Epernay Cedex
Tel: 00 33 (0)3 26 51 19 30
Fax: 00 33 (0)3 26 55 19 79
Internet site: www.champagne.fr
- Syndicat Général des Vignerons
de la Champagne
44 Av. Jean-Jaurès - BP 176
51205 Epernay Cedex
Tel: 00 33 (0)3 26 59 55 00
Fax: 00 33 (0)3 26 54 97 27
Internet site:
www.champagnesdevignerons.fr
- Union des Maisons de Champagne
1 rue Marie-Stuart – BP 2185
51081 Reims Cedex
Tel: 00 33 (0)3 26 47 26 89
Fax: 00 33 (0)3 26 47 48 44
Internet site: www.umc.fr

RIQUEWIHR

(Alsace) – page 20

Principal appellations
produced in the commune:
Alsace Grand Cru Schoenenbourg;
Alsace Grand Cru Sporen;
Alsace Riesling; Alsace
Gewurztraminer; Alsace Tokay-Pinot
Gris; Alsace Pinot Noir; Alsace Muscat

Tourist Information:
Office du Tourisme
2 rue de la Première-Armée-
Française
68340 Riquewihr
Tel: 00 33 (0)3 89 49 08 40
Fax: 00 33 (0)3 89 49 08 49

Syndicats viticoles:
- Syndicat des Vignerons
Récoltants d'Alsace
rue Jean-Mermoz
68015 Colmar Cedex
Tel: 00 33 (0)3 89 41 97 41
Fax: 00 33 (0)3 89 23 01 97
- Conseil Interprofessionnel
des Vins d'Alsace
Maison des Vins d'Alsace
12, Av. de la Foire-aux-Vins
68012 Colmar Cedex
Tel: 00 33 (0)3 89 20 16 20
Fax: 00 33 (0)3 89 20 16 30
Internet site: www.vinsalsace.com

ROQUEBRUN

(Languedoc) – page 102

Principal appellation
produced in the commune:
St-Chinian

Tourist Information:
Office du Tourisme
Avenue des Orangers
34460 Roquebrun
Tel: 00 33 (0)4 67 89 79 97
E-mail: otroquebrun@bechamail.com

Cave coopérative viticole:
Cave de Roquebrun
Avenue des Orangers
34460 Roquebrun
Tel: 00 33 (0)4 67 89 64 35
Fax: 00 33 (0)4 67 89 57 93

ST-EMILION

(Bordeaux) – page 132

Principal appellations
produced in the commune:
St-Emilion; St-Emilion Grand Cru;
St-Emilion Grand Cru Classé;
St-Emilion Premier Grand Cru Classé

Tourist Information:
Office du Tourisme
Place des Créneaux
33330 St-Emilion
Tel: 00 33 (0)5 57 55 28 28
Fax: 00 33 (0)5 57 55 28 29

Syndicats viticoles:
- Conseil Interprofessionnel
des Vins de Bordeaux
1 Cours du 30-Juillet
33075 Bordeaux Cedex
Tel: 00 33 (0)5 56 00 22 66
Fax: 00 33 (0)5 56 00 22 77
E-mail: civb@vins-bordeaux.fr
- Le Collège des Vins de St-Emilion
rue Guadet - BP 15
33330 St-Emilion
Tel: 00 33 (0)5 57 55 50 52
Fax: 00 33 (0)5 57 55 53 10

Caves coopératives viticoles:
- Union de Producteurs
de St-Emilion
1 rue Goudichaux
33330 St-Emilion
Tel: 00 33 (0)5 57 24 70 71
Fax: 00 33 (0)5 57 24 65 18
- Cave de Puisseguin
Lussac St-Emilion - 33570 Lussac
Tel: 00 33 (0)5 57 55 50 40
Fax: 00 33 (0)5 57 74 57 43

Museum:
Musée de la Bouteille
2 rue du Couvent - 33330 St-Emilion
Tel: 00 33 (0)5 57 24 70 20

ST-MACAIRE

(Bordeaux) – page 136

Principal appellations
produced in the commune:
Côte de Bordeaux St-Macaire;
Bordeaux

Tourist Information:
Office du Tourisme
8 rue du Canton - 33490 St-Macaire
Tel: 00 33 (0)5 56 63 32 14
Fax: 00 33 (0)5 56 76 13 24

Syndicat viticole:
Conseil Interprofessionnel
des Vins de Bordeaux
1 Cours du 30-Juillet
33075 Bordeaux Cedex

Tel: 00 33 (0)5 56 00 22 66
Fax: 00 33 (0)5 56 00 22 77
E-mail: civb@vins-bordeaux.fr
Cave coopérative viticole:
Cave des Côtes de Bordeaux St-Macaire
33490 St-Pierre-Aurillac
Tel: 00 33 (0)5 56 63 54 84
Fax: 00 33 (0)5 56 62 37 94

St-Pourçain-sur-Sioule
(Centre) – page 156
Principal appellation
produced in the commune:
St-Pourçain
Tourist Information:
Office du Tourisme
13 Place Maréchal Foch
03500 St-Pourçain-sur-Sioule
Tel: 00 33 (0)4 70 45 94 30
Fax: 00 33 (0)4 70 45 94 05
Cave coopérative viticole:
Union des Vignerons de St-Pourçain
Quai de la Ronde - BP 27
03500 St-Pourçain-sur-Sioule
Tel: 00 33 (0)4 70 45 42 82
Fax: 00 33 (0)4 70 45 99 34
Museum:
Musée de la Vigne et du Terroir
1, Cour des Bénédictins
03500 St-Pourçain-sur-Sioule
Tel: 00 33 (0)4 70 45 62 07

St-Roman-de-Bellet
(Nice) – page 90
Principal appellation
produced in the commune:
Bellet
Tourist Information:
Office du Tourisme
Aéroport Nice Côte Azur - 06200 Nice

Sancerre
(Centre) – page 158
Principal appellation
produced in the commune:
Sancerre
Tourist Information:
Office du Tourisme
Nouvelle Place - 18300 Sancerre
Tel: 00 33 (0)2 48 54 08 21
Fax: 00 33 (0)2 48 78 03 58
E-mail: ot.sancerre@wanadoo.fr
Syndicats viticoles:
- Bureau Interprofessionnel
des Vins du Centre
9 Route de Chavignol
18300 Sancerre
Tel: 00 33 (0)2 48 78 51 07
Fax: 00 33 (0)2 48 78 51 08
E-mail: bivc@wanadoo.fr
- UVS (Union Viticole Sancerroise)
9 Route de Chavignol
18300 Sancerre
Tel: 00 33 (0)2 48 78 51 03
Fax: 00 33 (0)2 48 78 51 04
E-mail: uvs@wanadoo.fr
Cave coopérative viticole:
La Cave des Vins de Sancerre
Avenue de Verdun - 18300 Sancerre
Tel: 00 33 (0)2 48 54 19 24
Fax: 00 33 (0)4 48 54 16 44

Saumur
(Loire Valley) – page 148
Principal appellation
produced in the commune:
Saumur; Saumur-Champigny;
Coteaux de Saumur; Saumur Brut;
Crémant de Loire; Anjou
Tourist Information:
Office du Tourisme
Place Bilange – BP 241
49418 Saumur
Tel: 00 33 (0)2 41 40 20 60
Fax: 00 33 (0)2 41 40 20 69
Syndicats viticoles:
- Syndicat des Coteaux de Saumur
25 rue de la Paleine
49260 St-Cyr-en-Bourg
Tel: 00 33 (0)2 41 51 61 04
Fax: 00 33 (0)2 41 51 65 34
- Syndicat d'Appellation Saumur
Rouge
1 rue des Ducs-d'Aquitaine
49260 Le Puy-Notre-Dame
Tel: 00 33 (0)2 41 52 24 46
Fax: 00 33 (0)2 41 52 39 96
Cave coopérative viticole:
Les Vignerons de Saumur
Route du Mureau
49260 St-Cyr-en-Bourg
Tel: 00 33 (0)2 41 53 06 08
Fax: 00 33 (0)2 41 51 69 13

Sauternes
(Bordeaux) – page 138
Principal appellation
produced in the commune:
Sauternes
Tourist Information:
Office du Tourisme
11 rue Principale - 33210 Sauternes
Tel: 00 33 (0)5 56 76 69 13
Fax: 00 33 (0)5 57 31 00 67
Syndicats viticoles:
- Conseil Interprofessionnel
des Vins de Bordeaux
1 Cours du 30-Juillet
33075 Bordeaux Cedex
Tel: 00 33 (0)5 56 00 22 66
Fax: 00 33 (0)5 56 00 22 77
E-mail: civb@vins-bordeaux.fr
- Syndicat Viticole de Sauternes
Place de la Mairie - 33210 Sauternes
Tel: 00 33 (0)5 56 76 60 37
Fax: 00 33 (0)5 56 76 69 67

Savennieres
(Loire Valley) – page 152
Principal appellations
produced in the commune:
Savennières;
Savennières Coulée de Serrant;
Savennières Roche-aux-Moines;
Anjou; Anjou-Villages
Tourist Information:
Mairie/Office du Tourisme:
4 rue de la Cure
49170 Savennières
Tel: 00 33 (0)2 41 72 85 00
Syndicat viticole:
Syndicat des Producteurs
des Vins de Savennières

Château d'Epire
49170 Savennières
Tel: 00 33 (0)2 41 77 15 01
Fax: 00 33 (0)2 41 77 16 23

Seguret
(Rhône Valley) – page 68
Principal appellations
produced in the commune:
Côtes du Rhône-Villages Séguret;
Côtes du Rhône
Tourist Information:
Mairie/Office du Tourisme:
rue des Poternes
84110 Séguret
Tel: 00 33 (0)4 90 46 91 06
Fax: 00 33 (0)4 90 46 82 33
Syndicat viticole:
Comité Interprofession des Vins AOC
Côtes du Rhône et Vallée du Rhône
Hôtel du Marquis de Rochegude
6 rue des Trois-Faucons
84024 Avignon
Tel: 00 33 (0)4 90 27 24 00
Fax: 00 33 (0)4 90 27 24 09
E-mail: maison@vivarhone.com
Cave coopérative viticole:#i#
Les Vignerons de Roaix-Séguret
84110 Séguret
Tel: 00 33 (0)4 90 46 91 13
Fax: 00 33 (0)4 90 46 94 59

Solutre-Pouilly
(Burgundy) – page 40
Principal appellations
produced in the commune:
Pouilly-Fuissé; Mâcon; Mâcon-
Villages
Tourist Information:
Mairie / Office du Tourisme:
Le Bourg - 71960 Solutré-Pouilly
Tel: 00 33 (0)3 85 35 81 90
Fax: 00 33 (0)3 85 35 88 07
Syndicat viticole:
Syndicat du Cru Pouilly-Fuissé
71960 Solutré-Pouilly
Tel: 00 33 (0)3 85 35 81 88
Fax: 00 33 (0)3 85 35 82 92

Vaux-en-Beaujolais
(Burgundy) – page 44
Principal appellations
produced in the commune:
Beaujolais; Beaujolais-Villages
Tourist Information:
Mairie/Office du Tourisme:
Le Bourg - 69460 Vaux-en-Beaujolais
Tel: 00 33 (0)4 74 03 20 07
Fax: 00 33 (0)4 74 03 26 54
Syndicat viticole:
Inter Beaujolais
210, Blvd Vermorel
69661 Villefranche Cedex
Tel: 00 33 (0)4 74 02 22 10
Fax: 00 33 (0)4 74 02 22 19
E-mail:
interbeaujolais@beaujolais.net
Musée de la Vigne et du Vin:
Cave de Clochemerle
69460 Vaux-en-Beaujolais
Tel: 00 33 (0)4 74 03 26 58

Vezelay
(Burgundy) – page 36
Principal appellations
produced in the commune:
Bourgogne Vézelay; Bourgogne
Tourist Information:
Office du Tourisme
rue St-Etienne
89450 Vézelay
Tel: 00 33 (0)3 86 33 23 69
Fax: 00 33 (0)3 86 33 34 00
Syndicat viticole:
Bureau Interprofessionnel des Vins
de Bourgogne (Chablis/Auxerrois)
Le Petit Pontigny
1 rue de Chichée BP - 31
89800 Chablis Cedex
Tel: 00 33 (0)3 86 42 42 22
Fax: 00 33 (0)3 86 42 80 16
E-mail: bivb.Chablis@bivb.com
Cave coopérative viticole:
La Vézelienne
89450 Vézelay
Tel: 00 33 (0)3 86 33 29 62
Fax: 00 33 (0)3 86 33 35 03

Vougeot
(Burgundy) – page 38
Principal appellation
produced in the commune:
Clos de Vougeot
Tourist Information:
Mairie/Office du Tourisme:
rue du Vieux-Château
21640 Vougeot
Tel: 00 33 (0)3 80 62 86 14
Fax: 00 33 (0)3 80 62 82 99
Museum:
Château du Clos de Vougeot
rue de la Montagne
21640 Vougeot
Tel: 00 33 (0)3 80 62 86 09

Vouvray
(Loire Valley) – page 154
Principal appellations
produced in the commune:
Vouvray; Vouvray Pétillant
Tourist Information:
Mairie/Office du Tourisme:
12 Route Rabelais
37210 Vouvray
Tel: 00 33 (0)2 47 52 70 48
Fax: 00 33 (0)2 47 52 67 76
Syndicat viticole:
Syndicat Viticole du Vouvray
Vallée Chartier
37210 Vouvray
Tel: 00 33 (0)2 47 52 63 07
Fax: 00 33 (0)2 47 52 65 59
Cave coopérative viticole:
Cave des Producteurs de Vouvray
38 Vallée Coquette
37210 Vouvray
Tel: 00 33 (0)2 47 52 75 03
Fax: 00 33 (0)2 47 52 66 41

Picture Sources

- Archipel studio: pages 16b, 26b, 42b, 52b, 54b, 56a, 60b, 66, 69, 82b, 104, 110b, 116a, 126b, 128b, 138b, 150
- Nicole Colin: map on page 4
- DIAF:
G. Biolay: page 120
Tristan Deschamps: pages 158-159
Jean-Paul Garcin: pages 63, 102-103, 109, 110a
J-C. Gérard: pages 32-33
Gérard Gsell: pages 88-89
Rosine Mazin: pages 64-65
Camille Moirenc: pages 62, 70-71, 77, 87
Erwan Quemere: pages 98-99
Jacques Sierpinski: pages 6, 48a, 54a, 97, 119
Patrick Somelet: pages 54-55,
Jean-Daniel Sudres: pages 28-29, 43, 142, 142-143, 146, 152-153, 154-155
Daniel Thierry: pages 31, 36-37, 39
- Friedrich Gier: pages 16, 24, 25, 26a, 26-27, 34-35, 38, 146-147, 149, 160
- Vincent Lyky: pages 8b, 14, 46b, 48b
- Musée du Tire-Bouchon (Corkscrew Museum): page 86a

- SCOPE:
Louis Audoubert: page 123
Jean-Luc Barde: pages 17, 40, 41, 42a, 44ab, 45, 50-51, 52a, 52-53, 68, 94-95, 96, 104-105, 106-107, 108-109, 111, 112-113, 113, 114, 114-115, 116b, 117, 118, 120-121, 122, 124, 125, 130, 132-133, 134ab, 134-135, 138a, 156, 157
Philippe Blondel: pages 36, 66-67, 140, 154
Isabelle Eshraghi: pages 8a, 9
Daniel Gorgeon: pages 82-83
Michel Gotin: pages 14-15
Jacques Guillard: pages 10a, 11, 12ab, 12-13, 16a, 18, 18-19, 20, 20-21, 21, 22-23, 28b, 29, 30-31, 35, 46a, 47, 49, 50, 56b, 57, 58-59, 60a, 61, 68-60, 72, 102, 143, 144a, 148, 150-151, 152, 160-161
Michel Guillard: pages 10b, 126a, 126-127, 128a, 128-129, 131, 132, 136-137, 138-139, 144b, 158
Noël Hautemanière: page 105
Francis Jalain: pages 147
Michel Plassard: pages 141
- Jacques Veyroust: page 28a